Quesadillas

Over 100 Fast, Fresh, and Festive Recipes!

Steven and Katherine Ramsland

PRIMA PUBLISHING

PRIMA PUBLISHING and colophon are registered trademarks of Prima Communications, Inc.

Library of Congress Cataloging-in-Publication Data

Ramsland, Steven.
     Quesadillas : over 100 fast, fresh, and festive recipes! / by Steven and Katherine Ramsland.
        p. cm.
     Includes index.
     ISBN 0-7615-0544-X
     1. Quesadillas. I. Ramsland, Katherine. II. Title.
TX836.R36 1996
641.8'15—dc20   96-15833
                                                 CIP

97 98 99 00 01 HH 10 9 8 7 6 5 4 3 2 1

Printed in the United States of America

How to Order
Single copies may be ordered from Prima Publishing, P.O. Box 1260BK, Rocklin, CA 95677; telephone (916) 632-4400. Quantity discounts are also available. On your letterhead, include information concerning the intended use of the books and the number of books you wish to purchase.

Visit us online at http://www.primapublishing.com

Contents

3

APPETIZER QUESADILLAS   31

4

SEAFOOD QUESADILLAS   47

5

POULTRY AND MEAT QUESADILLAS   75

6

VEGETABLE QUESADILLAS   109

7

DESSERT QUESADILLAS   131

8

SALSAS, SAUCES, AND PESTOS   147

Introduction

Innovative Southwestern cuisine is one of the hottest trends in dining today. Although it has roots in Mexican fare, today's Southwestern cooking blends Creole, Asian, and Continental influences with native Southwestern ingredients to form a new and unique cuisine.

The quesadilla is a traditional Mexican food made of cheese and other ingredients sandwiched between two flour tortillas. It provides a perfect medium for blending a wide range of ingredients to create simple, flavorful, and quick meals. Much like the recent transformation of pizza from its traditional form to more upscale versions, quesadillas are now being cleverly recast by imaginative Southwestern restaurants into a whole new cuisine.

Like the "California-style" pizza, quesadillas are fun to make and perfect for experimenting with blends of Southwestern, Mexican, Japanese, Italian, Creole, and other diverse cuisines of America. In fact, since they are easier and faster to make than pizzas, we must ask why they have yet to reach the heights of pizza's popularity? Maybe it is because most people still associate quesadillas with the bland, overly cheesy variety served in Mexican restaurant chains. The quesadillas you will learn to make from this book should forever banish from your mind images of the old, high-fat, uninspired version.

Today's quesadilla, like today's California-style pizza, is light and uses fresh, high-quality vegetables, fruits, poultry, herbs, cheese, and seafood. Some of our quesadillas are a meal on their own, while others are better served as appetizers, hors d'oeuvres, entrées, or desserts. Many can be made quickly, using ingredients found in a well-stocked pantry. Others will challenge you to take the time to prepare them properly and then slowly savor their complex flavors with a bottle of fine wine.

This book offers a comprehensive guide to making all types of innovative quesadillas. On the following pages you will find information on the common *and* special ingredients necessary for creative quesadillas, with sections devoted to flours, cheeses, chiles, herbs, fruits, vegetables, oils, vinegars, condiments, and cooking equipment. Special cooking techniques, such as roasting peppers and garlic, handling chiles, and toasting nuts are included, along with tips for serving and preparing perfect quesadillas.

You will also find step-by-step instructions for making your own basic flour tortillas, along with recipes for whole wheat, multi-grain, corn, sweetened, nut-based, and liqueur-flavored tortillas. Tips are given for purchasing and storing tortillas, assembling and cooking quesadillas, and for garnishing and presentation.

We have also included a chapter devoted to various accompaniments to enjoy with quesadillas. Recipes include both traditional and modern salsas, sauces, and relishes made with basic ingredients such as tomatoes, chiles, tomatillos, corn, black beans, avocadoes, and a variety of fruit.

We hope that in learning and trying the recipes in this book, you will not only eat well and healthfully, but be inspired to create your own quesadilla recipes.

1

The Basics

History

Translated literally, quesadillas are *cheese cakes,* made either with corn or flour tortillas. Tortilla means *little cake,* and is a thin, round flatbread, baked or fried. Originally tortillas were always made from corn soaked in lime or ash. The soaking process would break down the hulls before the kernels were ground into a cornmeal flour. After the Spanish introduced wheat to the Native American culture, flour tortillas became more common. Since they are at once more delicate in flavor and durable in texture, they work better than corn tortillas for some purposes. The next chapter provides step-by-step instructions for making flour, corn, whole wheat, oat, and sweet dessert-style tortillas.

Cheese

The basic ingredient that all quesadillas share is the cheese, and there are many types of cheese available. Most quesadillas traditionally use a Monterey Jack or Cheddar; however the recipes in this book use a variety of melting cheeses, grating cheeses, and specialty cheeses—alone or combined.

Melting Cheeses

Melting cheeses are of vital importance to making quesadillas. The melted cheese enables the tortillas to stick to the ingredients and hold them together in a "sandwich." The many types of melting cheeses range from mild to sharper flavors. In general, we use a mild cheese, such as mozzarella or Monterey Jack, in a subtly flavored quesadilla. In other cases, we use a strongly flavored cheese that will stand up to, and complement, other bold ingredients. And in some recipes, we combine several cheeses to achieve a greater richness than any one cheese can achieve on its own.

Monterey Jack: Developed in Monterey County, California, during the nineteenth century by Scotsman David Jacks, this is now the staple cheese of quesadillas.

Cheddar: A moderately hard cheese, it varies in taste from mild to sharp, depending on its age.

Fontina: A moderately hard yellow cheese, it has a slightly nutty flavor and a strong aroma. Most fontina cheese comes from Denmark or Italy; we generally prefer the somewhat milder Danish variety.

Havarti: A cream-enriched cow's milk cheese, Havarti is semi-soft, with small holes and a buttery taste.

Gouda: A moderately hard, smooth cheese, Gouda has a mild, creamy, slightly nutty flavor. It is widely available smoked.

Jarlsberg: A moderately hard, smooth Norwegian cheese with large holes and a strong, nutty flavor. Jarlsberg is also available smoked.

Mozzarella: The classic pizza melting cheese, it plays a major role in our quesadillas too. Mozzarella comes in a variety of types: part-skim-milk mozzarella; whole-milk mozzarella; and fresh, or "buffalo," mozzarella. We also use smoked mozzarella in several recipes.

Grating Cheeses

We generally use grating cheeses together with melting cheeses to provide more depth and character in the quesadilla. Grating cheeses have a sharper taste than the milder melting cheeses. Shaved grating cheeses can also make a simple and flavorful garnish when scattered over the dish.

Parmesan: A very hard, dry, crumbly cheese with a sharp, nutty flavor. The best Parmesan is labeled *Parmigiano-Reggiano.* Buy it whole rather than grated; it is worth the extra price.

Asiago: Semi-soft to hard, depending on age, Asiago is an Italian cheese with a mild to sharp flavor.

Specialty Cheeses

By using some of the following cheeses, we break the traditional mold for quesadillas. Many specialty cheeses are especially useful in appetizers and desserts.

Goat Cheese: Gourmet stores and well-stocked supermarkets now provide a wide variety of domestic and imported goat cheeses. Lower in fat than cow's milk cheese, these cheeses have a unique flavor that varies by brand and style. Fresh goat cheese generally has a light taste; the aged variety has a more tangy flavor. Some goat cheeses are marinated in olive oil and herbs for added dimension. In general, use a high-quality goat cheese, either domestic or French.

Brie: Creamy Brie and Camembert are mild, creamy cheeses that we tend to use in appetizer quesadillas. They pair especially well with fruits and nuts.

Blue Cheeses: A wide variety of richly flavored blue cheeses are readily available in markets. We generally prefer English Stilton.

Ricotta: Widely available in grocery stores, ricotta is an Italian cheese made from the whey drained from the curds that go into mozzarella and provolone. It is a fresh, smooth, mild cheese of loose consistency that is spooned and spread, or dotted onto the tortillas. As with mozzarella, ricotta comes in both part-skim and whole-milk varieties.

Boursin: A French-style creamy cheese, it has a mild taste, and usually comes mixed with garlic and herbs, or with black pepper.

Mascarpone: An Italian cheese-related product made with heavy cream that has been lightly fermented and thickened. Mascarpone is usually used in desserts, such as tiramisù, and we use it in dessert quesadillas.

Although some of the cheeses suggested in the recipes are high in fat, many come in lowfat varieties, such as Jarlsberg, mozzarella, ricotta, and Cheddar. However, unlike the overly gooey quesadillas you have probably eaten in restaurants, the quesadillas in this book generally use only as much cheese as is necessary to hold the tortillas together. The dessert quesadillas use more cheese for richer taste. Feel free to experiment with adding extra cheese, or using less, according to your dietary needs and tastes.

Chiles

Although our quesadillas sometimes wander far from their southwestern roots, we do use traditional chiles in many of our recipes, both for quesadillas and salsa. Many varieties of chiles, fresh, dried, and canned, are available these days in well-stocked grocery stores. Our staple chiles include:

Anaheim: Usually pale green, tapered, about 5 to 6 inches long with a pointed tip, these are the mildest of the fresh green chiles.

Jalapeño: Medium to dark green, tapered to a round end, about 1 1/2 to 3 inches long, these range from moderate to very hot. We use them fresh, roasted, and in the dried and smoked form known as chipotle chile. The chipotle form is extremely hot, with a smoky flavor that is great in sauces, in crema, and in decorative "paints."

Poblano: Dark green, tapered to a point, with shoulders 3 to 4 inches around, and 4 to 5 inches long. Poblanos are generally medium hot, and are always used cooked or roasted.

Serrano: Bright green or red, thin, and about 1 1/2 to 2 inches long. Generally hotter than the more commonly known jalapeño, the serrano is used extensively in salsa, either fresh or roasted.

If you have difficulty finding a specific chile in your supermarket, you can make some substitutions between the chiles listed above. For example, if you're having a hard time locating serranos, you can substitute the somewhat milder jalapeño. Although they vary in heat intensity, in certain recipes you can use the Anaheim instead of the poblano. In some recipes, canned green chiles can replace fresh roasted chiles. Just be careful about substituting a hotter chile for a milder chile, or you could be in for a surprise. And never use green bell peppers in place of any of the chiles listed.

NOTE: Be very careful, when handling fresh chiles, not to touch your face or eyes before thoroughly washing your hands. Better yet—wear rubber gloves.

Dried, powdered chile varies greatly in quality and taste. Look for a pure ground chile without the cumin, garlic, salt, etc. that is added to most commercial powder. Try to find a high-quality ancho (sometimes called pasilla) chile powder, an authentic Hungarian paprika, New Mexican, or molido chile.

Herbs, Fruits, and Vegetables

Avocados: We prefer the bumpy-skinned, darker Haas variety of avocado to the smoother, green variety. Plan ahead when using avocados, since they are usually sold before they are ripe. A ripe avocado should be slightly soft to the touch.

Black Beans: We prefer to use black beans to other varieties. Black beans are native to Central and South America and have a strong, smoky flavor. Some newer varieties need little or no presoaking and cook up in 60 to 90 minutes. In a pinch, you can use cooked, canned black beans, but be sure to rinse them well first.

Cilantro: Also known as fresh coriander or Chinese parsley, cilantro is a staple of Southwestern cooking, and the most commonly used herb in our recipes. Also common to Asian cuisines, cilantro is the most widely used herb in the world. It resembles flat-leaf parsley, but has a much more flavorful, aromatic, sweet taste. Try to find it with its roots still attached; its leaves should look fresh, green, and unwilted. Store it either with the roots covered by water or wrapped in paper towels in the refrigerator. When cooking with cilantro, only use the leaves and discard the stems. Do not substitute coriander seed or ground coriander for fresh cilantro.

Garlic: We like to roast garlic, which mellows its sometimes overwhelming flavor, resulting in a sweeter, nuttier flavor. When using fresh garlic, remove the skins and crush the individual cloves with the flat side of a large chef's knife, then mash or mince.

Ginger: A rhizome, or root, native to Asia, it is now often imported from the Caribbean. More typically used in Asian or Caribbean cuisines, ginger is great when used in certain marinades and salsas. When grating ginger, peel off the skin and use the fine holes on a box grater. There are also special ginger graters available in Asian markets.

Limes: Try to find either Mexican or Florida Key limes, as they are sweeter when ripe than other varieties. Lime juice is used extensively in salsa and, of course, in those margaritas you'll want to sip with your quesadillas.

Mangoes: Introduced to the United States through Brazil in the early eighteenth century, mangoes are widely available in supermarkets. A ripe mango has a smooth yellow and red skin and is tender to the touch. Its flavor is both sweet and tart, with hints of melon, papaya, banana, and pineapple. We use the mango as a core ingredient in several quesadillas, as well as in salsa.

Mushrooms, Wild: Wild mushroom varieties, such as chanterelles, morels, and porcini, have an intense, earthy flavor that goes well in Southwestern dishes. In quesadilla recipes with an Asian influence we use shiitake and oyster mushrooms. All are readily available in well-stocked supermarkets.

Olives: Several of our quesadilla recipes make extensive use of olives. We prefer the strong, tangy flavor of such Mediterranean olives as the dark kalamata olives from Greece or the smaller oil-cured niçoise olives from France. Canned domestic black olives are generally too bland to be of much interest in our quesadillas.

Onions: When they are in season, we prefer to use sweet Vidalia, Maui, or Walla Walla onions for our quesadillas and salsas. In general, you will want to use the sweetest onions available for salsa, since you don't want sharp raw onions to overpower the other ingredients.

Papayas: A tropical fruit with pink flesh, a mottled yellow-green skin, and a gourd-like shape. They have a sweet, citrus-banana flavor and are often used in salsas and desserts.

When ripe, papayas are yellow and tender to the touch. Their flavor is enhanced with a touch of fresh lime juice.

Pepper, Black: Try to always use freshly ground pepper, as its flavor is superior to preground varieties. Black peppercorns should have a strong, fresh aroma, and are best bought in gourmet shops.

Pine Nuts: Also known as pignoli or piñones, pine nuts are native to the Southwest, where they grow at high elevations on evergreen piñon trees. Resembling corn kernels, most commercially sold pine nuts today come from Europe and China. They are great eaten raw, toasted, or ground into a flour for desserts.

Shallots: Members of the onion family, shallots have a papery reddish-brown skin and an elongated shape. Their taste is a cross between an onion and garlic.

Tomatillos: Cultivated by the Aztecs, tomatillos look like small green tomatoes covered with a papery husk. Used frequently in Southwestern cooking, the tomatillo has a tart, green apple–green tomato flavor that sweetens when roasted. Fresh tomatillos should be bought when green and firm, with dry, clean husks.

Tomatoes: Always use the freshest tomatoes available for our quesadillas and salsas. Generally, we prefer the Roma tomato, as it has more pulp and less juice than most other varieties. When used in sauces, always seed and skin tomatoes. Sun-dried tomatoes are usually available in three varieties: a very dry, brittle variety that must be reconstituted in hot water before use; a flexible, chewy-dry variety; and a marinated version packed in oil. In general, we prefer not to use the marinated tomatoes unless we want to use the oil for a specific purpose.

Zucchini: Best used when 6 inches in length or smaller, the zucchini is also known as the courgette. It has medium- to dark-green skin and a pale yellow–white flesh. It can be used in salsa and has a wonderful flavor when grilled.

Oils, Vinegars, and Condiments

Butter: Always use unsalted butter when cooking, as it tastes fresher and gives you better control over the flavor of the food. However, since salt acts as a preservative, it is best to store any unused unsalted butter in the freezer. If you prefer the taste of salted butter, just remember to cut down on the amount of salt in the recipe.

Caribbean Jerk Seasoning: With the increasing popularity of Caribbean cooking, a wide variety of jerk sauces can be found in major supermarkets and specialty food stores. Jerk seasonings come in both liquid and dry-rub, and are used for marinating and grilling meats or fish. They are generally fiery hot, although some are tempered with a sweetness. Busha Browne's and Pickapeppa are two popular brands.

Hoisin Sauce: A thick sauce made from soybeans, vinegar, and spices, hoisin sauce is used for marinades and barbecue sauces. It is available in the Asian section of most large grocery stores.

Olive Oil: Sometimes our recipes call for "extra-virgin olive oil" and sometimes just "olive oil." Extra-virgin olive oil is made from the first pressing of the olives. It is intensely fruity and fragrant, and it is more expensive than virgin olive oil. Since it loses its character when cooking, it is best used in salsa and in recipes where you want to savor its hearty flavor. Regular olive oil or virgin olive oil is made from the second and subsequent pressings, and is useful for cooking or marinades. It is what we refer to when recipes simply call for olive oil.

Sesame Oil: We use the dark, richly flavorful Asian sesame oil in marinades and certain Southwest-Asian quesadillas.

Tahini: We use this sesame-seed paste in certain marinades. It is available in health food stores and well-stocked grocery stores.

Tamari: A Japanese soy sauce that is somewhat thicker than the Chinese-style soy sauce. We primarily use tamari in marinades.

Vinegars: Vinegars are used in this book mostly in marinades and in salsas. Rice vinegar is a light Japanese vinegar with a subtle flavor that goes well in fruit salsa, such as avocado or mango salsa. Apple cider vinegar is the most commonly used vinegar in Southwestern cuisine for its clear, fruity flavor. Balsamic vinegar, made from aged Italian red wine, is full, flavorful, and goes well with tomato salsa.

Special Equipment and Techniques

You really don't need much in the way of special equipment to make quesadillas or salsa, although a few items can make your life easier. The most essential tools of any kitchen are a good chef's knife and a sharp paring knife. If you know how to use them, these two knives will help you prepare foods as quickly, and with more precision, than a food processor. However, many cooks prefer food processors, which are indispensable for making sauces and pestos. But for most salsas, stick with the knives.

If you make your own tortillas (and we hope you will!), a tortilla press is a lot easier to use than a rolling pin and a couple of plates. We use an electric model that presses and cooks the tortillas in one step, but we provide instructions for other methods.

For heating quesadillas, a flat cast iron griddle is the easiest way to go. The *comal* is the traditional Mexican cooking surface. Large, round, and flat, it is made either glazed or unglazed, fired clay or cast iron. Although the *comal* seems to give a better crust to the tortilla, it is not as widely available as the cast-iron griddle.

Many of our recipes require grilling foods. If you use an outdoor gas grill, as many of us do, try experimenting with the variety of wood chips readily available. You will get a more traditional, smoky flavor if you use mesquite, hickory, pecan, or another variety of wood chip, yet still have the convenience of gas.

Since you will be grating cheese for each quesadilla, make sure you've got a decent cheese grater, or a grating attachment for your food processor. A box-style grater is an easy and versatile piece of equipment. For semi-soft cheeses, the larger shredding holes work best; for hard cheeses, go with the small grating holes.

A kitchen scale is a handy, inexpensive tool that will help you to achieve the right proportions in your cooking, especially if you're multiplying or splitting recipes. For the most part, we give the measurements of cheese, meats, poultry, and fish in ounces. However, if you don't have a kitchen scale, 1 ounce of cheese is usually equivalent to about $1/4$ cup of shredded cheese. Most of the quesadilla recipes call for 3 to 4 ounces of cheese, or $3/4$ to 1 cup of shredded cheese.

Here are a few essential cooking techniques that may be unfamiliar.

Handling Chiles and Removing Seeds and Stems

Many of our recipes call for removing the seeds and stems of the chiles, because that is where the heat is, and we use chiles more for flavor than for pure heat. When handling chiles, try to avoid contact with the oils. Always thoroughly wash your hands with soap immediately afterward, and never bring your hands up to your face or eyes until cleaned. Many cooks prefer to wear rubber gloves when handling chiles and use a plate rather than a cutting board to avoid getting the oils into the cut surface of the wood or plastic. Remove the seeds and ribs by gently scraping or cutting with a sharp paring knife.

For larger chiles and bell peppers, cut a hole around the stem and pull the ribs and seeds out. Slice open and scrape away the remaining seeds and ribs.

Roasting Peppers and Chiles

Roasting chiles and bell peppers both mellows and enriches their flavors. You can roast chiles and peppers on a gas stove or a barbecue grill, or in an oven broiler or dry skillet. The quickest method is on a grill or gas burner. Using a pair of tongs, turn the peppers so that they blister and char evenly over high heat. When the entire surface is blackened, place the peppers in a plastic bag or a bowl covered with plastic wrap and let them steam for 10 minutes. Then peel the skin away, cut them open, and remove the seeds.

If you are roasting several peppers, an oven broiler can be an efficient method. Place the peppers on the grid of a broiler pan about 4 inches from the flame. Turn them frequently until blackened, remove, and steam as above.

The dry skillet method works best with smaller chiles such as jalapeños or serranos, but should not be used with larger chiles or bell peppers, as they would tend to stew in their liquid. Heat a heavy skillet on medium-high. Add the chiles and turn them frequently until done. Skin and seed as above.

Regardless of the method used, make sure you pull the skins off with your fingers, with the help of a paring knife. Do not wash off the skin under running water, as you will dilute the natural oils and flavor. Since roasted chiles will generally keep in the refrigerator for several days, you may want to roast several chiles or peppers at once to speed your cooking for the next few days.

Rehydrating and Puréeing Dried Chiles

Rehydrating and puréeing dried chiles is a common technique in Southwest cooking. The puréed chiles are used for sauces, cremes, and salsas. The dried chiles most commonly used in our recipes are the *chipotle*—the smoked, dried form of the *jalapeño*—and the *ancho*—the dried form of the *poblano* chile. To rehydrate a dried chile, first stem, seed, and dry-roast it in a heavy skillet or *comal* for 3 to 4 minutes. Shake the chiles a few times to prevent burning. Remove the chiles from the skillet and cover with water in a small pan. Bring the water to a boil, turn the heat off, and let the chiles soak for 15 to 20 minutes. Remove the chiles from the water and purée in a blender with enough of their cooking water to achieve the desired consistency.

Roasting Garlic

Roasting garlic adds a slightly sweet, mellow flavor to foods without overpowering them, as unroasted garlic sometimes does. Roasted garlic can also be spread on breads or served as a side dish.

To roast garlic, keep the papery outer skin on the garlic head. With a sharp chef's knife, cut the top third of the garlic head off. Place the garlic head on a sheet of aluminum foil (or in a clay garlic roaster) and drizzle with 1 tablespoon of olive oil. Close the foil and roast for 45 minutes in a 375 degrees F oven until tender and buttery.

An alternative method is to break up the garlic head into individual unpeeled cloves and dry roast in a *comal* or heavy skillet over low heat for 45 minutes. Shake the garlic a few times and adjust the heat, as necessary, to ensure that the garlic does not brown.

Peeling and Seeding Tomatoes

The easiest way to peel and seed tomatoes is to cut out the stem and slash an *X* into the bottom of the tomato. Immerse the tomato in boiling water for 30 seconds, then plunge it in icy water until cool enough to handle. The skin should pull away easily. Cut the tomato in half crosswise and squeeze to remove the seeds.

Toasting Nuts

Toasting brings out the full flavor of nuts, so you may want to do this where recipes call for nuts. Simply spread the nuts on a baking sheet and heat in 350 degrees F oven until lightly browned.

Black Beans

Although you can buy canned black beans, they can also easily be made at home—and you don't have to soak them overnight. Depending on their freshness, you can cook black beans in 60 to 90 minutes.

Makes about 4 cups

2	cups dried black beans
1	tablespoon olive oil
1	small onion, diced
3	cloves garlic, minced
2	teaspoons ground cumin
2	jalapeño chiles, seeded, deribbed, and minced
1/2	teaspoon pure chile powder
1/2	teaspoon dried oregano
1	small bunch cilantro
1/2	teaspoon salt

Rinse the beans and check for stones. Heat the olive oil in a large pot, add the onion, and cook until slightly browned. Add the garlic, cumin, jalapeños, chile powder, and oregano, and cook for 1 minute. Add the beans and cilantro, and enough water to cover. Bring to a boil, then reduce heat and simmer gently, adding water as necessary, until the beans are tender, about 60 to 90 minutes. Add the salt, remove the cilantro, and check the tenderness of the beans. Cook a little longer and, if necessary, adjust the seasoning.

Serve drained.

To serve as a sauce, purée about half the beans and return them to the pot. Add 1/4 cup tomato purée and 1 tablespoon fresh lime juice. Thin, if necessary, with water or stock. Adjust seasonings, and serve.

Tips for Preparing and Serving Quesadillas

Unless otherwise noted, the quesadilla recipes in this book will serve four adults as an appetizer or two adults as a main course. For the sake of simplicity, each recipe is for one quesadilla. If you're serving more people, or you have big appetites, adjust the recipes upward. Dessert recipes serve two to four people, using smaller tortillas.

Quesadillas are sometimes assembled with one tortilla placed on top of another, sometimes folded over like half-moons, and sometimes open-faced, like a pizza. We typically lightly brown the quesadillas on a stovetop skillet. However, if you are preparing several quesadillas for a party, it is easier to brown them for 5 to 7 minutes in a 350 degrees F oven.

Serve quesadillas by cutting them into wedges and presenting them either on a large plate or divided among individual plates. In either case, you'll want to garnish quesadillas with some salsa, sour cream, cilantro, or another decorative edible. Throughout the book we suggest appropriate salsa pairings and garnishes to aid in your presentation. The key is to be creative, and serve your quesadillas with a little artistic flair.

Try the recipes as we have written them, but feel free to experiment as well. If you cannot get a certain ingredient, substitute something that excites you. Adjust the amount of chiles to achieve the level of heat that you like. We generally avoid making quesadillas with a lot of cheese, but add more if that's what you like. Or if you do not like a particular cheese we suggest, try another one, or several together. Quesadillas are quick, casual, and adaptable to a wealth of ingredients. So have fun, and enjoy your quesadillas!

2

Tortillas

Tortillas are flat, thin, feathery light "cakes" of corn or flour, and are a staple in Southwestern cooking. They are indispensable in making quesadillas. Both flour and corn tortillas are widely available in grocery stores throughout the United States, and many are of good quality and flavor. However, unless you buy your tortillas freshly made from a local tortilla store, packaged tortillas do not compare to the flavor and consistency of home-made tortillas, so we would like to encourage you to make your own.

Homemade tortillas are so easy to prepare that once you have tasted the difference, you may never want to buy tortillas again. And since leftover tortillas freeze well, you can make a big batch on a slow day and use the tortillas later.

We have included recipes for a variety of traditional and *nouvelle* tortillas that you can make at home. In general, flour tortillas are the easiest to make and the ones you'll use most often. Corn tortillas take a little practice, but for some recipes they provide a richness of flavor that help "make" the quesadilla. Whole wheat and oat tortillas are reminiscent of "mountain" or pita bread. We really stretch the limits of tortilla-making with our shortbread, nut, and flavored tortillas for desserts.

Flour Tortillas

Most of our quesadilla recipes call for 8- to 10-inch flour tortillas, as these are the most versatile and seem to work best. The basic recipe and technique for flour tortillas provides the foundation for making whole wheat, oat, shortbread, and flavored tortillas.

Be sure to keep the dough moist by keeping it covered with plastic wrap while you are cooking the tortillas. If you allow the dough to dry, your tortillas will end up heavy and crumbly rather than light. Flip the tortillas frequently while they are cooking to keep them from drying out and becoming too crisp. If the tortilla puffs up while cooking, simply press down lightly with a spatula.

Traditional recipes for flour tortillas use lard or hard vegetable shortening. We prefer to use vegetable oil in some tortillas, or butter for its flavor and richness.

Basic Flour Tortillas

Makes 12 (8- to 10-inch) tortillas

2   cups unbleached all-purpose flour
1/2   teaspoon salt
1/2   teaspoon baking powder
1/4   cup unsalted butter, vegetable oil, or vegetable shortening
2/3   cup warm water

Mix the flour, salt, and baking powder in a large bowl. Thinly slice the butter and add to the dry ingredients. Using your fingertips, rub the ingredients together into coarse crumbs. Add the water all at once and continue mixing with a fork until the mixture has the consistency of stiff bread dough. If a bit too dry, add a little extra water; if too moist, add a little extra flour. Do not overmix.

Divide and shape the dough into 12 golf ball–size pieces. Cover with plastic wrap and let rest for 30 to 60 minutes.

Roll out the rested dough balls into circles 8 to 10 inches in diameter and 1/8 inch thick, or shape using a tortilla press. Be sure to form and cook the tortillas one at a time, keeping the remaining dough covered and moist.

Cook the tortillas on a hot, ungreased griddle, *comal,* or cast-iron pan over medium-high heat for about 1 minute, turning frequently, until no longer translucent. Remove from heat and keep warm under a tea towel while you cook the remaining tortillas.

Whole Wheat Tortillas

Makes 12 (8- to 10-inch) tortillas

1	cup unbleached all-purpose flour
1	cup whole wheat flour
1	teaspoon salt
$3/4$	teaspoon baking powder
$1/4$	cup unsalted butter, vegetable oil, or vegetable shortening
$2/3$	cup hot water

Mix and cook the tortillas using the directions for Basic Flour Tortillas, provided on page 19.

Oat Bran Tortillas

Makes 12 (8- to 10-inch) tortillas

1 1/2 cups unbleached all-purpose flour
1/2   cup oat bran flour
1   teaspoon salt
3/4   teaspoon baking powder
1/4   cup unsalted butter, vegetable oil, or vegetable shortening
2/3   cup hot water

Mix and cook the tortillas using the directions for Basic Flour Tortillas, provided on page 19.

Red Chile Tortillas

Makes 12 (8- to 10-inch) tortillas

2   cups unbleached all-purpose flour
1   teaspoon salt
3/4 teaspoon baking powder
1/4 cup unsalted butter, vegetable oil, or vegetable shortening
2/3 cup warm water
2   tablespoons dried chile purée (ancho, guajillo, New Mexico Red, or pasilla, page 12)

Mix the flour, salt, and baking powder in a large bowl. Thinly slice the butter and add to the dry ingredients. Using your fingertips, rub the ingredients together into coarse crumbs. Combine the water and the chile purée, and pour into the dry mixture all at once. Mix with a fork or a wooden spoon until the ingredients are incorporated and the mixture has the consistency of stiff bread dough. If a bit too dry, add a little extra water; if too moist, add a little extra flour. Do not overmix.

Form and cook the tortillas according to the instructions for Basic Flour Tortillas, provided on page 19.

Corn Tortillas

Corn tortillas are traditionally made with *masa*, a fresh corn dough that has great flavor, but is not commonly available for home use. Typically, homemade corn tortillas are made with *masa harina,* corn that has been soaked in lime or ash to break down the hulls before the kernels are ground into a fine corn-meal flour. It is not the same as cornmeal, which is simply ground corn. It is said that the soaking process used in making *masa harina* enriches the cornmeal by releasing protein and minerals locked in the kernels. You can find *masa harina* either in the baking section or the Latin American section of most supermarkets.

Corn tortillas are a bit trickier to make than flour tortillas, so it'll probably take you a few efforts before you start to get it right. If you prefer, several good brands of commercially made corn tortillas are available in supermarkets.

Corn Tortillas

Makes 16 small (8-inch) tortillas

2   cups *masa harina*
$1/2$ teaspoon salt
1   cup warm water
$1^1/2$ tablespoons vegetable oil (optional)

Mix all the ingredients together in a large bowl, using your hands or a wooden spoon, until the dough is thick and smooth. Cover the dough with plastic wrap while you make the tortillas.

To form the tortillas, pull or scoop a golf ball–size piece from the dough. Keeping the unused dough covered and moist, place the ball between 2 sheets of plastic wrap on a tortilla press (or between 2 plates) and press down to achieve the thinness and diameter that you desire.

If the tortilla dough sticks to the plastic wrap, add a little more *masa harina* to the remaining dough. If it crumbles, add a little more water until you get the consistency you want. Shape the rest of the dough into golf ball–size pieces, and cover with plastic wrap to keep moist.

Cook each tortilla on a hot, ungreased griddle, *comal,* or cast-iron pan over medium-high heat until stiffened, about 30 seconds. Turn over and cook for 1 minute or less, then turn again for a few seconds. The tortilla should be slightly browned but still pliable. Remove from heat and keep warm under a tea towel while you cook the remaining tortillas.

Dessert Tortillas

Dessert tortillas range from sweet, buttery versions of traditional flour tortillas to sweet, nutty tortillas that are close cousins to cookies. Here we provide you with several recipes that we use in our dessert quesadillas.

Shortbread Tortillas

Makes 10 (6- to 8-inch) tortillas

$3/4$ cup unbleached all-purpose flour
3   tablespoons granulated sugar
6   tablespoons unsalted butter, melted

Place the flour in a medium-size bowl. Mix the sugar and butter in a large measuring cup until the sugar has dissolved. Add to the flour and mix until the ingredients are thoroughly combined. Form and cook the tortillas using the directions for Basic Flour Tortillas, provided on page 19.

Chocolate Tortillas

Makes 8 (6-inch) tortillas

1	cup unbleached all-purpose flour
2	tablespoons granulated sugar
2	tablespoons cocoa powder
3	tablespoons unsalted butter, melted
1/2	cup warm water

Blend together the flour, sugar, and cocoa in a large bowl. Cut in the butter until the mixture resembles coarse crumbs, and then gradually mix in the water. Knead with fork or fingers until the dough is smooth and well blended. It should be slightly sticky.

Cover dough with plastic and let rest at least 30 minutes. When ready, roll out the dough balls into circles 6 to 8 inches in diameter and 1/8 inch thick, or shape using a tortilla press. Be sure to form and cook the tortillas one at a time, keeping the remaining dough covered and moist. You may need to dip your rolling pin in flour to prevent dough from sticking.

Cook the tortillas on a hot, ungreased griddle, *comal*, or cast-iron pan, turning frequently, for about 1 minute in all, until firm but not stiff. Remove from heat and keep warm under a tea towel while you cook the remaining tortillas.

Nut Tortillas (Macadamia, Hazelnut, or Almond)

Makes 8 (6-inch) tortillas

2/3   cup nuts (macadamia, hazelnut, or almond)
2/3   cup granulated sugar
2/3   cup unbleached all-purpose flour
6   tablespoons unsalted butter, melted, or a nut-flavored oil
1   egg
2   tablespoons warm water
1   teaspoon vanilla extract

Preheat oven to 375 degrees F. Grease a large cookie sheet. Combine nuts, sugar, and flour in food processor fitted with a metal blade and process into a powder. Do not overprocess or the nuts will turn into a "butter." Add the butter, egg, water, and vanilla. Blend for 30 seconds.

Drop batter 1 tablespoon at a time onto the prepared cookie sheet. Use the back of a spoon to spread the clumps into thin, round cookies 6 inches in diameter, separating cookies by 1 inch.

Bake for 10 minutes until edges are golden and crisp. Use a spatula with a thin edge to remove from cookie sheet and place on a paper towel to cool.

To store, place between sheets of waxed paper in an airtight container.

Liqueur-Flavored Tortillas

You can make wonderfully flavored tortillas using liqueurs, fruit oils, or extracts. Simply make a sweetened flour tortilla with your favorite flavoring mixed in with the water. Here we provide a recipe for an orange-flavored tortilla using pure orange oil, available in gourmet stores.

Makes 6 (8- to 10-inch) tortillas

1	cup unbleached all-purpose flour
2	tablespoons granulated sugar
1/2	teaspoon salt
2	tablespoons unsalted butter, cold
1/2	cup warm water
1/4	teaspoon pure orange oil

Mix the flour, sugar, and salt in a large bowl. Thinly slice the butter and add to the dry ingredients. Using your fingertips, rub the ingredients together into coarse crumbs. Combine the water and the orange oil. Add the liquid to the dry mixture all at once and continue mixing with a fork until the dough has the consistency of stiff bread dough. If dry and crumbly, add a little extra water; if too moist, add a little extra flour. Do not overmix.

Divide and shape the dough into 6 golf ball–size pieces. Cover with plastic wrap and let rest for 30 to 60 minutes. When ready, roll out the dough balls into circles 8 to 10 inches in diameter and $^1/_8$ inch thick, or shape using a tortilla press. Form and cook the tortillas one at a time, keeping the remaining dough covered and moist, and be sure to wash your hands immediately with strong soap, as the orange oil can cling to skin and sting your eyes.

Cook the tortillas on a hot, ungreased griddle, *comal,* or cast-iron pan over medium-high heat, turning frequently, for about 1 minute in all, until no longer translucent. Remove from heat and keep warm under a tea towel while you cook the remaining tortillas.

3

Appetizer
Quesadillas

We know that quesadillas of all kinds are served in restaurants as appetizers—you really can use almost any recipe in this book as an appetizer rather than an entrée. Even so, it seems that some quesadillas are better served only as appetizers or hors d'oeuvres, and these are the recipes we include in this chapter.

Our appetizer quesadillas typically use specialty cheeses, such as goat cheese or Brie, and they are often paired with fruit, such as mangoes or papayas. We also offer quesadilla versions of food combinations often seen in appetizers, such as smoked salmon with goat cheese or boursin cheese and tomatoes. We even have a quesadilla based on the classic summertime appetizer of fresh mozzarella and tomatoes with basil and olive oil.

If you plan to serve a quesadilla as "finger food," then be careful not to overfill it with ingredients. Keep the quesadilla thin with nothing running out the edges. Also, make sure you heat the quesadilla long enough to get a nice, crisp crust.

Bon Appetit!

French Gourmandise Walnut

We discovered this French semi-soft cheese laced with chopped walnuts in a local specialty store. When spread on a warm, fresh flour tortilla, this makes a simple yet elegant appetizer.

2   fresh (8-inch) flour tortillas
2   to 3 ounces French Gourmandise walnut cheese
1   sweet apple, sliced

Spread the Gourmandise over half of each tortilla and fold over to create 2 half-moon quesadillas.

Heat a pan or griddle over medium heat and cook the quesadillas for 2 to 3 minutes on each side until they lightly brown and the cheese melts. Remove from the pan and cut each quesadilla into 4 pieces. Serve with apple slices on the side.

Three Cheeses and Roasted Hazelnuts

This quesadilla makes a great appetizer. The slightly sweet, nutty flavor of the roasted hazelnuts pairs perfectly with the mellow blend of three cheeses. It also goes well with a fruit-based salsa, especially raspberry or peach.

2	fresh (8-inch) flour tortillas
1/4	cup shredded Monterey Jack cheese
1/4	cup shredded Gouda cheese
1/4	cup shredded Jarlsberg cheese
1/4	cup chopped roasted sweet hazelnuts (*bresilienne*)
1/3	serrano chile, roasted, peeled, seeds and stem removed, and finely minced
1	tablespoon finely minced Vidalia or other sweet onion
1	tablespoon minced fresh cilantro
	Salt and freshly ground black pepper
1/4	cup salsa of choice
1	to 2 cilantro sprigs for garnish

In a large bowl, combine the Monterey Jack, Gouda, Jarlsberg, hazelnuts, serrano chile, onion, and cilantro, and season with salt and pepper. Sprinkle the mixture over 1 of the tortillas, cover with the second tortilla, and press down lightly.

Heat a pan or griddle over medium heat, and cook the quesadilla for 2 to 3 minutes on each side until it lightly browns and the cheese melts. Remove quesadilla from the pan and cut it into appetizer-size wedges. Garnish with the salsa and cilantro sprigs.

Sun-Dried Tomato and Roasted Garlic Pesto with Arugula

We use the Sun-Dried Tomato and Roasted Garlic Pesto in several quesadilla recipes. Here the sweet-smoky vibrancy of the pesto is paired with arugula, shallots, and a blend of smoothly mild cheeses.

2	fresh (8-inch) flour tortillas
1	teaspoon olive oil
1	shallot, minced
1	bunch arugula (approximately 1 cup, packed)
2	ounces Danish fontina cheese, shredded
1	ounce Monterey Jack cheese, shredded
1/4	cup Sun-Dried Tomato and Roasted Garlic Pesto (page 160)
	Salt and freshly ground black pepper
2	tablespoons sour cream for garnish
2	tablespoons chopped Italian parsley for garnish

In a small saucepan, heat the olive oil over high heat. Add the minced shallots and sauté for 1 to 2 minutes until translucent. Add the arugula and stir-fry for another minute until wilted. Remove from heat and set aside.

Combine the fontina and Monterey Jack and sprinkle half on 1 tortilla. Crumble and scatter the pesto evenly over the tortilla, followed by the arugula mixture and the remainder of the cheese. Season with salt and pepper to taste. Cover with the second tortilla, and press down lightly.

Heat a pan or griddle over medium heat, and cook
the quesadilla for 2 to 3 minutes on each side until it lightly
browns and the cheese melts. Remove the quesadilla from the
pan and cut it into appetizer-size wedges. Garnish with the sour
cream topped with a sprinkling of pesto. Scatter the parsley
over the quesadilla and serve.

Mango, Vidalia Onion, Roasted Hazelnuts, and Brie

The rich sweetness of fresh mango and roasted hazelnuts is balanced by the onion, a little roasted jalapeño, and, of course, the creaminess of the Brie.

2 fresh (8-inch) flour tortillas
4 ounces Brie cheese at room temperature
1/2 fresh mango, peeled and diced
3 tablespoons chopped roasted sweet hazelnuts (bresilienne)
1 tablespoon finely minced Vidalia, Maui, or other sweet onion
1/2 jalapeño chile, roasted, peeled, seeds and stems removed, and finely minced
1 tablespoon minced fresh cilantro
1 tablespoon sour cream for garnish

Remove the rind from the Brie and spread the cheese on each tortilla.

Reserve 1 tablespoon of the mango and 1 tablespoon of the hazelnuts. In a large bowl, combine the remaining mango and hazelnuts with the onion, jalapeño, and cilantro. Spread the mango mixture evenly over 1 tortilla, and cover with the second tortilla (cheese-side in).

Heat a pan or griddle over medium heat, and cook the quesadilla for 2 to 3 minutes on each side until golden brown. Remove the quesadilla from the pan and cut it into appetizer-size wedges. Garnish with the sour cream topped by the reserved mango. Scatter the reserved hazelnuts over the quesadilla and serve.

NOTE: Chopped roasted sweet hazelnuts, also called *bresilienne,* are available in gourmet food stores.

Brie, Papaya, and Serrano Chile

This quesadilla provides a great combination of sweet and hot flavors, topped by the creaminess of Brie. Try this with whole wheat or oatbran tortillas.

2	fresh (8-inch) flour tortillas
3	tablespoons minced fresh cilantro
6	ounces Brie cheese at room temperature
1/2	ripe papaya, peeled and diced (approximately 3/4 cup)
1	serrano chile, seeds and stems removed, and finely minced
2	tablespoons sour cream for garnish

Reserve 1 tablespoon of the cilantro for garnish.

Remove the rind from the Brie and spread the cheese evenly over 1 tortilla. Randomly scatter the papaya, chile, and 2 tablespoons cilantro over the top. Cover with the second tortilla and press down lightly.

Heat a pan or griddle over medium heat, and cook the quesadilla for 2 to 3 minutes on each side until it lightly browns and the cheese melts. Remove the quesadilla from the pan and cut it into appetizer-size wedges. Place on individual plates and garnish with the sour cream and reserved cilantro.

Brie, Mango, and Poblano Chile

This recipe is similar to the one with Brie and papaya, but with a different fruit–chile combination. Make sure the mango is ripe. The easiest way to dice a mango is to cut it in half lengthwise, along each side of the flat pit in the center. Remove the pit and, with the skin still on, cut dice marks in the mango's flesh. Pick up the mango, push up on the skin, and slice off your diced pieces of mango.

2   fresh (8-inch) flour tortillas
3   tablespoons minced fresh cilantro
6   ounces Brie cheese at room temperature
1/2 medium fresh mango, peeled and diced
1   poblano chile, roasted, seeds and stems removed, and
     finely minced
2   tablespoons sour cream for garnish

Reserve 1 tablespoon cilantro for garnish.

Remove the rind from the Brie and spread the cheese evenly over 1 tortilla. Randomly scatter the mango, poblano chile, and 2 tablespoons cilantro over the top. Cover with the second tortilla and press down lightly.

Heat a pan or griddle over medium heat, and cook the quesadilla for 2 to 3 minutes on each side until it lightly browns and the cheese melts. Remove the quesadilla from the pan and cut it into appetizer-size wedges. Place on individual plates and garnish with the sour cream and reserved cilantro.

Monterey Jack, Mango, and Red Pepper–Almond Pesto

The rich sweetness of mango is tamed somewhat by the pesto in this recipe. Be sure to grill the quesadilla until it is crisp so that it does not get soggy from the mango.

2   fresh (8-inch) flour tortillas
1/3 cup Red Pepper–Almond pesto (page 162)
1/2 mango, peeled and chopped
3   to 4 ounces Monterey Jack cheese, shredded
1   tablespoon chopped fresh cilantro for garnish

Spread the pesto evenly over 1 tortilla and top with the mango and cheese. Cover with the second tortilla and press down lightly.

Heat a pan or griddle over medium-high heat, and cook the quesadilla for 2 to 3 minutes on each side until it lightly browns and the cheese melts. Remove the quesadilla from the pan and cut it into appetizer-size wedges. Garnish with the cilantro, and serve.

Olive Pesto and Feta Cheese

Here's a Greek twist on the quesadilla! We prefer to use briny Greek kalamata olives for the pesto, but be creative and try other types of olives too.

2   fresh (8-inch) flour tortillas
2   tablespoons olive pesto (page 161)
2   ounces feta cheese

Spread the pesto evenly over 1 tortilla. Crumble the feta over the pesto. Cover with the second tortilla and press down lightly.

Heat a pan or griddle over medium heat, and cook the quesadilla for 2 to 3 minutes on each side until it lightly browns and the cheese melts. Remove the quesadilla from the pan, cut it into appetizer-size wedges, and serve.

Smoked Salmon with Herbed Goat Cheese and Capers

Try to get a high-quality Norwegian, Scottish, or Pacific Northwest smoked salmon for this recipe. The Eddie Bauer company sells an excellent sockeye salmon smoked over aromatic alder fires. Use either a French or domestic herbed goat cheese, available in gourmet shops and well-stocked supermarkets.

2   fresh (8-inch) flour tortillas
1/2   cup water
1/4   cup sweet Vidalia or Maui onion, thinly sliced and slices halved
3   ounces fresh herbed goat cheese
4   ounces smoked salmon, thinly sliced
1   teaspoon drained capers
1   sprig dill for garnish

Heat the water in a medium skillet over high heat until boiling. Add the onion, cook for 30 seconds, remove from heat, and let stand for about 10 minutes, until the slices are wilted. Drain and set aside.

Spread half of the goat cheese over 1 tortilla. Lay the salmon over the cheese, and evenly distribute the onion and capers over the salmon. Spread the remaining cheese over the second tortilla, and sandwich the two tortillas together to form the quesadilla.

Heat a pan or griddle over medium heat, and cook the quesadilla for 2 to 3 minutes on each side until it lightly browns and the cheese melts. Remove the quesadilla from the pan and cut it into appetizer-size wedges. Garnish with the dill, and serve.

Boursin Cheese and Tomatoes

Boursin is a spreadable French cheese that generally comes in either an herb-garlic version or a black pepper version. For this recipe, we prefer the black pepper variety, but feel free to substitute herb-garlic boursin.

2   fresh (8-inch) flour tortillas
3   ounces black pepper boursin cheese
1   fresh tomato, thinly sliced

Spread the boursin evenly over 1 tortilla. Top with a single layer of tomato slices. Cover with the second tortilla and press down lightly.

Heat a pan or griddle over medium heat, and cook the quesadilla for 2 to 3 minutes on each side until it lightly browns and the cheese melts. Remove the quesadilla from the pan, cut it into appetizer-size wedges, and serve.

Fresh Mozzarella and Tomatoes with Basil and Olive Oil

Here's a summer classic with Italian origins. For this recipe you must use only fresh, high-quality ingredients. This quesadilla is best served open-faced.

2   fresh (8-inch) flour tortillas
1/4 cup shredded mozzarella cheese
2   Roma tomatoes, cut crosswise into 1/4-inch slices
1/4 pound fresh mozzarella cheese, cut into 1/4-inch slices
2   tablespoons fresh basil leaves, cut into chiffonade
     (thin strips)
1   tablespoon extra virgin olive oil
     Salt and freshly ground black pepper

Preheat oven to 375 degrees F.

Scatter the shredded mozzarella evenly over 1 tortilla set on a baking sheet. Cover with the second tortilla and press down lightly. Arrange a single layer of tomato slices over the sandwiched tortillas, followed by the fresh mozzarella slices. Scatter the basil leaves and drizzle the olive oil over the top of the open-faced quesadilla. Lightly salt and pepper to taste.

Carefully slide the quesadilla into the preheated oven and bake until it lightly browns and the cheese melts. Remove from oven, cut into appetizer-size wedges, and serve.

Stilton and Sautéed Walnuts

Stilton, the rich English blue cheese, paired with walnuts is a classic combination. Here we have put some spin on the classic combination by adding a little kick to the walnuts. If you cannot find Stilton, substitute another high-quality blue cheese.

2   fresh (8-inch) flour tortillas
1   teaspoon olive oil
1/4   cup finely chopped walnuts
1/2   teaspoon minced fresh thyme
1/8   teaspoon high quality red chile powder, such as ancho or molido chile
3   to 4 ounces Stilton cheese
1   sprig fresh thyme, for garnish

In a medium saucepan, heat the olive oil over medium heat. Add the walnuts, thyme, and chile powder. Stir for about 2 minutes, until the walnuts are lightly browned. Remove from heat and set aside.

Crumble 3 ounces of the Stilton over 1 tortilla. Evenly scatter the walnut mixture over the cheese. Cover with the second tortilla and press down lightly.

Heat a pan or griddle over medium heat, and cook the quesadilla for 2 to 3 minutes on each side until it lightly browns and the cheese melts. Remove the quesadilla from the pan, cut it into appetizer-size wedges, and serve. Garnish at the center with the reserved Stilton and the thyme sprig.

4

Seafood
Quesadillas

Although much of the Southwest is landlocked and seafood dishes are not considered a staple of the region's traditional cuisine, the widespread availability of fresh fish today has helped make seafood a prominent feature in modern Southwestern kitchens. This is especially true in Southern California, where you can find wonderful blends of Southwestern and Pacific Rim tastes, and along the Gulf Coast of Texas and into Louisiana, where a Creole influence comes through in the cooking.

Some of our seafood quesadillas reflect Asian and Creole influences, but you will also notice Caribbean, Chesapeake Bay, and European flavors here. Several of the recipes make use of sauces *within* the quesadilla, rather than salsa on the side. A great example of this is the Sambuca Shrimp quesadilla—one of our favorites!

Grilled Swordfish with Sweet Corn and Tomato Relish

Grilled swordfish is a real treat when not overcooked. Because it is so lean, it can dry out quickly. When grilling the fish for a quesadilla, remember to undercook it slightly, since it will cook a bit more on the stovetop.

2	fresh (8- to 10-inch) flour tortillas
2	tablespoons olive oil
1	clove garlic, minced
2	tablespoons minced cilantro
1	teaspoon freshly ground black pepper
1	(6- to 8-ounce) fresh swordfish steak, cut 1 inch thick
1	cup fresh sweet corn kernels (2 large ears of corn)
1/2	cup tomato, seeded and diced
1	serrano chile, seeds and stems removed, and minced
2	tablespoons unseasoned rice vinegar
1	tablespoon unsalted butter, cold, cut into pieces
1/2	teaspoon kosher or sea salt
3	to 4 ounces Monterey Jack cheese, shredded

In a small bowl mix the olive oil, garlic, 1 tablespoon of the cilantro, and 1/2 teaspoon of the black pepper. Coat the swordfish steak with this mixture and marinate at room temperature for at least 30 minutes.

Preheat your grill.

In a small bowl combine the corn, tomato, serrano chile, rice vinegar, butter, and the remaining 1 tablespoon of cilantro. Heat a small saucepan over moderate heat and add the corn mixture and remaining 1/2 teaspoon black pepper and salt. Stir until the butter melts. Cover and set aside while you grill the fish, reserving 1/4 cup of the relish for garnish.

Grill the swordfish over a hot fire for 3 to 4 minutes per side until done, but still pink in the center. Remove from heat and flake apart with a fork into bite-size pieces.

In a medium-size bowl combine the flaked swordfish, the corn-tomato relish, and the Monterey Jack. Spread evenly over 1 tortilla. Cover with the second tortilla and press down lightly.

Heat a pan or griddle over medium heat, and cook the quesadilla for 2 to 3 minutes on each side until it lightly browns and the cheese melts. Remove it from the pan and cut into wedges. Garnish with a loose mound of the corn-tomato relish.

Grilled Swordfish with Sun-Dried Tomatoes, Cilantro, and Havarti

We liven up the swordfish in this quesadilla with a spicy sun-dried tomato mixture.

2	fresh (8- to 10-inch) flour tortillas
2	tablespoons olive oil
1	clove garlic, minced
1	tablespoon unseasoned rice vinegar
3	tablespoons minced fresh cilantro
	Freshly ground black pepper
1	(6- to 8-ounce) fresh swordfish steak, cut 1 inch thick
3/4	cup shredded Havarti cheese (approximately 3 ounces)
1/3	cup sun-dried tomatoes, moist-style, roughly chopped
6	to 8 shakes hot sauce, such as Tabasco
	Salt
	Salsa of choice for garnish
	Sour cream for garnish

In a small bowl combine the olive oil, garlic, vinegar, and 1 tablespoon of the cilantro. Add 6 turns of the black pepper. Coat the swordfish steak with this mixture and marinate at room temperature for at least 30 minutes.

Preheat your grill.

Grill the swordfish over a hot fire for 3 to 4 minutes per side until done, but still pink in the center. Remove from heat and flake apart with a fork into bite-size pieces.

In a medium-size bowl combine the grilled swordfish, Havarti, sun-dried tomatoes, the remaining 2 tablespoons cilantro, and the hot sauce and salt to taste. Spread the mixture evenly over 1 tortilla. Cover with the second tortilla and press down lightly.

Heat a pan or griddle over medium heat, and cook the quesadilla for 2 to 3 minutes on each side until it lightly browns and the cheese melts. Remove it from the pan and cut into wedges. Garnish with salsa. We prefer sun-dried tomato or roasted tomato salsa and some sour cream.

Blackened Tilapia with Ginger, Scallions, and Red Pepper Sauce

Tilapia is a mild, slightly sweet freshwater fish that even appeals to people who normally dislike fish. It is usually sold in 4- to 6-ounce boneless fillets.

2	fresh (8- to 10-inch) flour tortillas
1	tablespoon unsalted butter
1	clove roasted garlic, mashed
1/2	teaspoon grated fresh ginger
1/4	red bell pepper, roasted, peeled, seeds and stem removed, and minced
2	tablespoons thinly sliced scallions
2	tablespoons heavy cream
1	teaspoon pure chile powder, such as ancho or molido chile
1	teaspoon freshly ground black pepper
1	teaspoon dried oregano
1	teaspoon granulated sugar
1/4	teaspoon ground cinnamon
1/4	teaspoon salt
1	(4- to 6-ounce) boneless tilapia fillet
1	tablespoon peanut oil
4	to 6 ounces Danish fontina cheese, shredded

Prepare the sauce by melting the butter in a small saucepan over moderate heat. Add the garlic, ginger, and red pepper, and cook for 1 minute. Add 1 tablespoon of the scallions and cook for 1 more minute. Increase the heat to high and add the cream. Stir until the sauce thickens enough to coat a spoon lightly. Remove from heat and set aside.

Prepare the blackening seasoning by combining the chile powder, black pepper, oregano, sugar, cinnamon, and salt. Just before cooking, dredge the tilapia fillet in the spices to coat.

Heat a cast-iron skillet over medium-high heat. Add the peanut oil, and when it starts to smoke, add the seasoned tilapia and cook quickly, 1 to 2 minutes per side until golden brown. Remove from heat and flake apart with a fork into bite-size pieces. Combine in a medium-size bowl with the red pepper sauce.

Scatter one half of the fontina over 1 tortilla, followed by the fish mixture, and top with the remaining cheese. Cover with the second tortilla and press down lightly.

Heat a pan or griddle over medium heat, and cook the quesadilla for 2 to 3 minutes on each side until it lightly browns and the cheese melts. Remove it from the pan and cut into wedges. Garnish with the remaining 1 tablespoon scallion slices.

Grilled Tuna with Wild Mushrooms, Ginger, and Fontina Cheese

This is another "sauced" quesadilla that seems to work so well with seafood. Use any type of wild mushrooms, or combine with white button mushrooms.

2	fresh (10-inch) flour tortillas
2	tablespoons unsalted butter
1 1/2	teaspoons minced shallots
3/4	cup sliced wild mushrooms
1/4	cup white wine
1	teaspoon grated fresh ginger
1	scallion, thinly sliced
	Salt and freshly ground black pepper
1	(4- to 6-ounce) tuna steak, approximately 1 inch thick
1	tablespoon olive oil
3	ounces Danish fontina cheese, shredded

Preheat your grill.

Heat 1 tablespoon of the butter in a medium sauté pan over medium-high heat, then add the shallots and cook for about 2 minutes. Add the mushrooms and cook for another 2 to 3 minutes, being careful not to brown the shallots. Add the wine and continue to cook until the liquid is reduced by two thirds. Remove from heat and stir in the remaining 1 tablespoon butter, ginger, and one half of the scallion. Salt and pepper to taste, and set aside.

Brush the tuna steak with the olive oil. Season with salt and pepper, and grill over a medium fire for 3 minutes per side until done, but still pink in the center. Remove from heat and flake apart with a fork into bite-size pieces.

In a medium-size bowl combine the tuna, mushroom sauce, and fontina. Scatter the mixture evenly over 1 tortilla. Cover with the second tortilla and press down lightly.

Heat a pan or griddle over medium heat, and cook the quesadilla for 2 to 3 minutes on each side until it lightly browns and the cheese melts. Remove it from the pan and cut into wedges. Garnish with the remaining scallion slices.

Grilled Swordfish with Roasted Red Peppers and Cilantro Pesto

With this recipe you can either roast the red peppers ahead of time or cut fresh red bell peppers into strips and grill them alongside the fish, until the skins are browned and the flesh tender.

2   fresh (10-inch) flour tortillas
1   tablespoon olive oil
1   teaspoon Dijon mustard
2   tablespoons minced fresh cilantro
      Salt and freshly ground black pepper
1   (4- to 6-ounce) swordfish steak, approximately 1 inch thick
3   ounces Havarti cheese, shredded
1   red bell pepper, roasted, seeds and stem removed, and cut into strips
3   tablespoons Cilantro Pesto (page 151)

In a bowl that can comfortably hold the fish, mix the olive oil, mustard, and 1 tablespoon minced cilantro. Salt and pepper the swordfish steak and place it in the marinade, turning to coat thoroughly. Marinate at room temperature for at least 30 minutes.

Preheat your grill.

Grill the fish over a medium fire for 3 to 4 minutes per side, until done, but still pink in the center. Remove from heat and flake apart with a fork into bite-size pieces.

Scatter one half of the Havarti evenly over 1 tortilla, followed by the fish and red pepper, and top with the remaining cheese. Spread 2 tablespoons of the Cilantro Pesto over the second tortilla, and press pesto-side down onto the first tortilla.

Heat a pan or griddle over medium heat, and cook the quesadilla for 2 to 3 minutes on each side until it lightly browns and the cheese melts. Remove it from the pan and cut into wedges. Garnish with the remaining 1 tablespoon Cilantro Pesto and 1 tablespoon minced cilantro.

Sambuca Shrimp

This is an absolutely delightful shrimp quesadilla with a European influence. One of our favorites! Sambuca is an anise-flavored Italian liqueur.

2	fresh (8- to 10-inch) flour tortillas
1	tablespoon unsalted butter
6	medium-large shrimp, peeled, deveined, and coarsely chopped
1	shallot, minced
1	tablespoon Sambuca liqueur
1	tablespoon dry vermouth
1/4	cup heavy cream
1/4	cup peeled, seeded, and chopped tomatoes
	Salt and freshly ground black pepper
2	to 3 ounces mozzarella cheese, shredded
2	scallion tops, chopped, for garnish

Heat the butter in a large sauté pan over moderate heat. When the foam subsides, add the shrimp, and sauté for 2 to 3 minutes. Add the shallots and cook, stirring, for 1 minute. Add the Sambuca and vermouth, and reduce by one half.

Add the cream, tomatoes, and salt and pepper to taste and cook until the sauce is thick and coats the spoon. Reserve 1 tablespoon of the sauce. Remove the pan from the heat, add the mozzarella, and stir until the cheese begins to melt. Spread this mixture over one half of each tortilla, folding the second half over the top. Heat a pan or griddle over medium heat, and cook both half-moon quesadillas for 2 to 3 minutes on each side until they lightly brown and the cheese melts. Remove them from the pan and cut into wedges. Drizzle the reserved Sambuca sauce lightly over each, and garnish with the scallion.

Jerk Shrimp with Sun-Dried Tomatoes, Vidalia Onion, and Creamy Havarti

The spicy flavors of the jerk seasoning and sun-dried tomatoes are offset in this quesadilla by the sweet onion and creamy cheese. Use a commercial jerk sauce, available in most well-stocked grocery stores, to marinate the shrimp.

2	fresh (8- to 10-inch) flour tortillas
1	teaspoon olive oil
1	tablespoon minced Vidalia onion
6	medium-large shrimp, peeled, deveined, and coarsely chopped
6	ounces Havarti cheese, shredded
1/4	cup sun-dried tomatoes, moist-style
1/4	cup minced fresh cilantro

Heat the olive oil in a large sauté pan over moderately high heat. Add the onion and shrimp and sauté for 2 to 3 minutes, or until pink and starting to curl. Remove from heat and combine in a medium-size bowl with the Havarti, sun-dried tomatoes, and 2 tablespoons of the cilantro. Scatter the shrimp mixture over 1 tortilla. Cover with the second tortilla and press down lightly.

Heat a pan or griddle over medium heat, and cook the quesadilla for 2 to 3 minutes on each side until it lightly browns and the cheese melts. Remove it from the pan and cut into wedges. Garnish with the reserved cilantro.

Grilled Shrimp, Vidalia Onions, and Fontina

Grilled Vidalia onions are an early-summer dining treat. Since the shrimp is also grilled in this recipe, this is a great quesadilla to make outside on the patio. You can substitute Maui, Walla Walla, or another variety of sweet onion for the Vidalia.

2   fresh (8- to 10-inch) flour tortillas

Marinade
1/4 cup olive oil
1   garlic clove, minced
1   tablespoon fresh lemon juice
1   tablespoon minced fresh cilantro
1   teaspoon freshly ground black pepper

6   to 8 whole medium-large shrimp, peeled and deveined
1   Vidalia onion, cut in 1/2-inch slices
1   tablespoon olive oil
     Salt and freshly ground black pepper
4   to 6 ounces Danish fontina cheese, shredded
     Salsa of choice for garnish such as Roasted Tomatillo (page 154)

Combine the marinade ingredients in a nonaluminum bowl. Add the shrimp and let marinate at room temperature for 1 hour.

Preheat your grill.

Remove the shrimp from the marinade and grill over a medium fire for about 3 minutes per side until pink and curled. Coat the onion slices with the olive oil. Salt and pepper the onions and grill until lightly caramelized. Coarsely chop the shrimp and onions.

In a medium-size bowl combine the shrimp, onion, and fontina. Scatter the mixture over 1 tortilla. Cover with the second tortilla and press down lightly.

Heat a pan or griddle over medium heat, and cook the quesadilla for 2 to 3 minutes on each side until it lightly browns and the cheese melts. Remove it from the pan and cut into wedges. Serve with salsa on the side.

Smoked Shrimp with Roasted Poblanos, Sun-Dried Tomatoes, and Goat Cheese

If you don't have a smoker, try using wood-smoking chips with your charcoal or gas grill, and cook the shrimp slowly over indirect heat.

2	fresh (8- to 10-inch) flour tortillas
2	tablespoons smoky barbecue sauce
1	tablespoon fresh lemon juice
1	serrano or jalapeño chile, seeds and stem removed, and diced
6	to 8 whole medium-large shrimp, peeled and deveined
1	poblano chile, roasted, seeds and stem removed, and chopped
1	tablespoon chopped sun-dried tomatoes, moist-style
4	ounces fresh, high-quality goat cheese
2	ounces mozzarella cheese, shredded
2	tablespoons minced fresh cilantro
1/4	cup Chipotle Crema for garnish (page 164)

Mix the barbecue sauce, lemon juice, and diced chile in a non-aluminum bowl. Coat the shrimp and let marinate at room temperature for 30 to 60 minutes.

Preheat your grill.

Grill the shrimp over a smoky fire for 3 minutes on each side. Coarsely chop the shrimp.

In a medium-size bowl combine the chopped shrimp, poblano chile, sun-dried tomatoes, goat cheese, mozzarella, and cilantro. Scatter the mixture evenly over 1 tortilla. Cover with the second tortilla and press down lightly.

Heat a pan or griddle over medium heat, and cook the quesadilla for 2 to 3 minutes on each side until it lightly browns and the cheese melts. Remove it from the pan and cut into wedges. Drizzle the Chipotle Crema over the top.

Sesame-Ginger Shrimp with Spinach

This quesadilla is inspired by the blend of ingredients in Chinese shrimp dumplings—but with a Southwestern twist!

2	fresh (8- to 10-inch) flour tortillas
1	teaspoon Asian sesame oil
6	to 8 medium-large shrimp, peeled, deveined, and coarsely chopped
4	ounces mozzarella cheese, shredded
1/4	cup well-drained, chopped, cooked spinach
1	teaspoon grated fresh ginger
1	tablespoon minced fresh cilantro
1	serrano chile, seeds and stem removed, and minced
1/4	teaspoon salt
1/4	cup Cilantro Crema for garnish (page 163)
4	to 6 chive stalks, chopped, for garnish

Heat the sesame oil on high in a medium sauté pan. Add the shrimp and sauté for 2 to 3 minutes until pink and starting to curl. Remove from heat and combine in a medium-size bowl with the mozzarella, spinach, ginger, cilantro, serrano chile, and salt.

Scatter the shrimp mixture evenly over 1 tortilla. Cover with the second tortilla and press down lightly.

Heat a pan or griddle over medium heat, and cook the quesadilla for 2 to 3 minutes on each side until it lightly browns and the cheese melts. Remove it from the pan and cut into wedges. Drizzle with the Cilantro Crema and top with a scattering of the chopped chives.

Maryland Crab Cake

Hey, why not? This recipe takes typical crab cake ingredients, but instead of mixing them with bread crumbs and egg to form a cake, we bind the ingredients with cheese and sandwich them between two tortillas! Old Bay is the seasoning mix traditionally used for seafood in the Chesapeake Bay area.

2	fresh (8- to 10-inch) flour tortillas
3/4	cup shredded Monterey Jack cheese
1/4	pound fresh lump crabmeat, picked over for shells and cartilage
2	tablespoons minced yellow onion
2	tablespoons minced red bell pepper
1	tablespoon minced fresh Italian parsley
1 1/2	teaspoons Worcestershire sauce
1/2	teaspoon Old Bay seasoning
1/4	teaspoon whole grain mustard
2	dashes hot sauce such as Tabasco
	Salt and freshly ground black pepper
	Seafood cocktail or tartar sauce

In a medium-size bowl thoroughly combine all of the ingredients except sauce. Scatter the mixture over one half of each tortilla, folding the second half over the top.

Heat a pan or griddle over medium heat, and cook both half-moon quesadillas for 2 to 3 minutes on each side until they lightly brown and the cheese melts. Remove them from the pan and cut into wedges. Serve with seafood cocktail or tarter sauce on the side.

Grilled Shrimp, Sun-Dried Tomatoes, and Ricotta

Sun-dried tomatoes, basil, and ricotta bring great traditional Italian tastes to a quesadilla. Blended with the spiciness of the jerked grilled shrimp, this quesadilla is sure to please.

2	fresh (10-inch) flour tortillas
12	to 16 whole small shrimp (about $1/2$ pound), peeled and deveined
$1/2$	cup jerk marinade
$1/4$	cup shredded Monterey Jack cheese
8	to 10 sun-dried tomato pieces, moist-style
$1/4$	cup shredded mozzarella cheese
$1/2$	cup ricotta cheese
6	to 8 fresh basil leaves, cut into thin strips (chiffonade)

Preheat your grill or broiler.

Combine the shrimp and jerk marinade in a nonaluminum bowl, turning the shrimp a few times to coat well. Let sit for about 15 minutes. Grill or broil for 2 to 3 minutes, turning once. Remove from heat, coarsely chop, and set aside.

Preheat the oven to 375 degrees F. Sprinkle a baking sheet with a little cornmeal.

Sprinkle the Monterey Jack evenly over 1 tortilla. Cover with the second tortilla and press down lightly. Evenly scatter the shrimp, sun-dried tomatoes, and mozzarella on top of the sandwiched tortillas, like a pizza. Dot with teaspoon-size clumps of the ricotta, and scatter the basil chiffonade over the top.

Place the quesadilla on the prepared pan and bake for 7 to 8 minutes until hot. Remove from the baking pan, cut into wedges, and serve.

NOTE: There are some wonderful Jamaican-style jerk marinades available in well-stocked supermarkets. Use a sweet-hot jerk sauce for this marinade.

Spicy Soft-Shell Crabs, Smoked Mozzarella, and Chipotle Crema

If we can make a crab cake quesadilla, why not a soft-shell crab quesadilla? If you're unsure how to clean the crabs, have the fishmonger clean them for you.

4	(6- to 8-inch) corn tortillas
1	egg
1/4	cup milk
3	tablespoons unbleached all-purpose flour
1 1/2	teaspoons ground cumin
1 1/2	teaspoons ground coriander
1/2	teaspoon powdered dried red chile (pasilla)
2	fresh soft-shell crabs, cleaned
2	tablespoons unsalted butter
4	to 6 ounces smoked mozzarella cheese, shredded
1/4	cup Chipotle Crema for garnish (page 164)
	Avocado Salsa (page 149)

In a medium-size bowl beat together the egg and milk. On a plate combine the flour, cumin, coriander, and chile. Dip the crabs in the egg wash and then dredge in the flour mixture.

Heat the butter in a large sauté pan over medium heat until foam subsides. Add the crabs shell-side down and cook for 3 to 5 minutes on each side, depending on the size of the crabs, until brown. Remove from the heat.

To assemble the quesadilla, sprinkle one quarter of the smoked mozzarella on each of 2 tortillas. Place the cooked crabs on top of the cheese, cover each with the remaining cheese, and top each with a tortilla.

Heat a pan or griddle over medium heat, and cook the quesadillas for 2 to 3 minutes on each side until they lightly brown and the cheese melts. Remove them from the pan and cut into wedges. Drizzle Chipotle Crema on each quesadilla, and serve with Avocado Salsa on the side.

NOTE: An easy way to flip over this, or any bulky quesadilla, is to slide the quesadilla onto a plate. Invert the pan over the plate and, using both hands, turn the pan and plate over so that the quesadilla is back in the pan.

Crab with Goat Cheese, Roasted Poblanos, and Toasted Pecans

Use only cooked fresh crab meat for this recipe, available at your local fish market or a good supermarket. If you want to cut corners on the expense, substitute claw meat for the lump crabmeat, but avoid canned crab or the imitation crab meat.

2   fresh (8- to 10-inch) flour tortillas
4   to 6 ounces high-quality, fresh, creamy goat cheese
1/2   pound fresh lump crabmeat, picked over for shells and
       cartilage
1   poblano chile, roasted, peeled, seeds and stems removed,
       and chopped
1/4   cup toasted chopped pecans
1   tablespoon minced fresh cilantro
       Black Bean and Roasted Corn Salsa (page 152) or
       Guacamole (page 150)

Break apart the goat cheese into small pieces and combine in a medium-size bowl with the crabmeat, poblano chile, pecans, and cilantro. Scatter the mixture over one half of each tortilla, folding the second half over the top.

Heat a pan or griddle over medium heat, and cook both half-moon quesadillas for 2 to 3 minutes on each side until they lightly brown and the cheese melts. Remove them from the pan and cut into wedges. Serve with salsa or guacamole—or both!—on the side.

Crab with Grilled Leek, Zucchini, and Roasted Garlic Crema

This quesadilla, like several others in this book, was inspired by the many crêpes we sampled while on a trip to Quebec, Canada.

2   fresh (8- to 10-inch) flour tortillas
1/2   small zucchini, cut into fine julienne
1/2   leek, white part only, cut into fine julienne
1   tablespoon olive oil
      Salt and freshly ground black pepper
1/2   pound fresh lump crabmeat, picked over for shells and cartilage
1/2   cup Roasted Garlic Crema (page 165)
4   to 6 ounces Havarti cheese, shredded

Preheat your grill.

Coat the zucchini and leek with the olive oil and season with salt and pepper. Using a specially designed vegetable grate, quickly grill seasoned zucchini and leek on a medium-hot fire until soft and slightly charred. Remove from heat.

In a medium-size bowl mix the crabmeat and 1/4 cup of the Roasted Garlic Crema.

Scatter one half of the Havarti over 1 tortilla. Cover with the crabmeat mixture. Scatter the grilled zucchini and leeks over the crab, followed by the remaining cheese. Cover with the second tortilla and press down lightly.

Heat a pan or griddle over medium heat, and cook the quesadilla for 2 to 3 minutes on each side until it lightly browns and the cheese melts. Remove it from the pan and cut into wedges. Drizzle with the remaining 1/4 cup Roasted Garlic Crema.

Scallops and Roasted Garlic Crema

In this recipe, the mild, sweet flavor of the pan-seared scallops are complemented by the sweet, nutty flavor of the Roasted Garlic Crema.

2	fresh (8- to 10-inch) flour tortillas
1	teaspoon olive oil
1/2	Vidalia or another small, sweet onion, finely chopped
6	sea scallops, rinsed and muscles removed
4	to 6 ounces Havarti cheese, shredded
1/2	cup Roasted Garlic Crema (page 165)

Heat the olive oil in a medium saucepan over medium heat. Add the onion and scallops and sauté for 4 to 6 minutes, stirring occasionally until golden. Remove from heat and chop coarsely.

In a medium-size bowl combine the scallop mixture with the Havarti and 1/4 cup of the Roasted Garlic Crema. Spread the mixture evenly over 1 tortilla. Cover with the second tortilla and press down lightly.

Heat a pan or griddle over medium heat, and cook the quesadilla for 2 to 3 minutes on each side until it lightly browns and the cheese melts. Remove it from the pan and cut into wedges. Drizzle with the remaining 1/4 cup Roasted Garlic Crema.

Pan-Seared Scallops with Cilantro Pesto and Sun-Dried Tomatoes

If you love cilantro, this quesadilla is for you! Try it with Black Bean and Roasted Corn Salsa.

2   fresh (8- to 10-inch) oatbran or flour tortillas
5   to 6 sea scallops, rinsed and muscles removed
1/4   cup Cilantro Pesto (page 151)
1/4   cup chopped sun-dried tomatoes, moist-style
4   ounces Monterey Jack cheese, shredded
       Black Bean and Roasted Corn Salsa (page 152)

Heat a nonstick sauté pan over medium-high heat and sear the scallops on all sides until cooked but still tender. Remove from heat and chop coarsely.

In a medium-size bowl, combine the scallops, Cilantro Pesto, sun-dried tomatoes, and Monterey Jack. Scatter evenly over 1 tortilla. Cover with the second tortilla and press down lightly.

Heat a pan or griddle over medium heat, and cook the quesadilla for 2 to 3 minutes on each side until it lightly browns and the cheese melts. Remove it from the pan and cut into wedges.

Garnish with a small mound of the salsa.

Bay Scallops with Sweet Red Pepper, Serrano Chile, and Hickory-Smoked Jarlsberg

This quick meal requires very little preparation, as the small bay scallops cook up in just a minute or two. Be careful not to overcook these scallops, or they will turn rubbery.

2	fresh (8- to 10-inch) flour tortillas
1/2	pound fresh bay scallops, rinsed and muscles removed
1 1/2	teaspoons Creole or Old Bay seasoning blend
1	tablespoon peanut oil
1/2	red bell pepper, seeds and stem removed, and finely chopped
1/4	cup minced yellow onion
1	serrano chile, seeds and stem removed, and minced
1	tablespoon minced fresh cilantro
3	ounces hickory-smoked Jarlsberg cheese, shredded
	Salsa of choice for garnish
	Sour cream for garnish

Rinse and drain the scallops, and then sprinkle evenly with the seasoning. Heat the oil in a large, heavy skillet over high heat. Add the scallops, red pepper, and onion and stir-fry for 1 or 2 minutes. Remove from heat.

In a medium-size bowl combine the scallop mixture with the serrano chile, cilantro, and Jarlsberg. Scatter the mixture over one half of each tortilla, fold in half, and press down lightly.

Heat a pan or griddle over medium heat, and cook both half-moon quesadillas for 2 to 3 minutes on each side until they lightly brown and the cheese melts. Remove them from the pan and cut into wedges. Serve with the salsa and sour cream on the side.

Poultry and Meat Quesadillas

Quesadillas made with beef, chicken, or pork can be found in any local Mexican eatery. And while we have included a few fairly traditional quesadillas in this chapter, the rest of our recipes provide very interesting ways to use these ingredients in quesadillas.

So, in addition to the classic Grilled Chicken and Monterey Jack quesadilla, we've got chicken quesadillas with toasted pecans and goat cheese, or with kalamata olives and creamy Havarti. For a more Asian slant, we've got Sesame-Ginger Chicken with Broccoli and Shallots; or Grilled Sesame Chicken with Shiitake Mushrooms.

For a very atypical Southwestern quesadilla, try our French-inspired Pork Tenderloin with Goat Cheese and Green Peppercorn Sauce. For an Indonesian slant, how about a quesadilla filled with pork-loin satay with grilled eggplant and scallions?

With all of our quesadillas, be sure to cut the meat or poultry into very small pieces, so that the flavors blend with the other ingredients and the quesadilla holds together well. Although quesadillas are often made with boldly flavored ingredients, the trick is to blend the ingredients so that you achieve consistency of taste with each bite. Besides, if the ingredients are cut too large, these quesadillas can really get messy!

Grilled Beef Tenderloin with Roasted Red Peppers and Stilton Cheese

The creamy, sharp flavor of the Stilton cheese combined with the roasted red pepper and grilled tenderloin make for a memorable taste combination. If possible, roast the red pepper and grill the beef over mesquite or some other smoky, flavorful fire. The quesadilla is grilled over the same fire to enhance its flavor.

2   fresh (10-inch) flour tortillas
1   red bell pepper
1 1/2 teaspoons commercial Southwest seasoning mix (or
     1/4 teaspoon *each* chile powder, paprika, cayenne, and
     ground cumin)
1   (4-ounce) filet mignon
1   ounce hickory-smoked Jarlsberg cheese, shredded
2   ounces Monterey Jack cheese, shredded
2   to 3 ounces Stilton cheese, crumbled
     Salt and freshly ground black pepper

Preheat your grill.

Roast the red bell pepper and close up in a paper bag. Sprinkle the Southwest seasoning over the filet and grill over a medium fire until medium-rare. Set aside to cool. Keep the grill moderately hot while you peel the roasted red pepper and remove its seeds and stem. Shred the pepper and grilled beef into roughly 2-inch-long pieces.

Scatter the Jarlsberg and Monterey Jack cheeses evenly over 1 tortilla. Cover with the second tortilla and press down lightly. Distribute the beef and red peppers strips lengthwise over the top of the sandwiched tortillas, like spokes on a wheel. Scatter the Stilton over all. Season with salt and pepper.

Carefully place the prepared quesadilla on a moderately hot, smoky grill until it lightly browns and the cheese melts. Remove from the grill, cut into wedges, and serve.

Sesame-Ginger Chicken with Broccoli and Shallots

This a great example of taking the quesadilla to the Pacific Rim!

2   fresh (8- to 10-inch) flour tortillas

Sesame-Ginger Marinade
2   tablespoons sesame oil
2   tablespoons grated fresh ginger
1   tablespoon tahini (sesame-seed paste)
1   tablespoon tamari
1 1/2   teaspoons light brown sugar
1   or 2 shakes hot sauce, such as Tabasco

1/2   (4-ounce) chicken breast, boneless and skinless
1   cup broccoli florets, coarsely chopped
1   tablespoon sesame oil
1   shallot, minced
2   scallions, minced
1 1/2   teaspoons tamari
2   ounces Danish fontina cheese, shredded
2   ounces light, mild Cheddar, shredded
2   tablespoons chutney, such as Major Grey, for garnish
1   scallion, sliced into small rings, for garnish

Combine all the marinade ingredients in a glass bowl or clear seal-top plastic bag. Add the chicken and marinate in the refrigerator for at least 2 hours. Preheat your grill.

Grill the chicken over a medium fire for 3 to 4 minutes per side until done. Set aside to cool slightly before shredding into bite-size pieces.

Blanch the chopped broccoli in salted water and set aside.

In a small saucepan heat the sesame oil over medium-high heat. Add the shallot and quickly sauté for 1 to 2 minutes.

In a medium-size bowl combine the chicken, broccoli, shallot, minced scallions, tamari, fontina, and Cheddar. Spread evenly over 1 tortilla. Cover with the second tortilla and press down lightly.

Heat a griddle or pan over medium heat, and cook for 2 to 3 minutes on each side until it lightly browns and the cheese melts. Remove it from the pan and cut into wedges. Garnish at the center with the chutney. Scatter the scallion slices over the quesadilla.

Grilled Sesame Chicken with Shiitake Mushrooms

This mild, subtly flavored quesadilla shows its obvious Asian influences. With this one, you'll want to savor each bite slowly, being careful not to overpower it with a salsa that is too boldly flavored.

2   fresh (8- to 10-inch) flour tortillas

Sesame-Tamari Marinade
1   tablespoon dark sesame oil
1   tablespoon tahini
1   tablespoon tamari
1 1/2 teaspoons light brown sugar
1   teaspoon molasses
1 1/2 teaspoons grated fresh ginger
1   clove garlic, minced

1   (6- to 8-ounce) whole chicken breast, boneless and skinless
1   tablespoon unsalted butter
1   shallot, minced
6   to 8 fresh shiitake mushrooms, sliced
     Salt and freshly ground black pepper
4   ounces mozzarella cheese, shredded
1   tablespoon toasted sesame seeds
1   scallion top, sliced into small rings, for garnish

Combine all the marinade ingredients in a glass bowl or clear seal-top plastic bag. Add the chicken and marinate in the refrigerator overnight, or at least for 2 hours. Preheat your grill.

Grill the chicken over a medium fire for 3 to 4 minutes per side until done. Set aside to cool slightly before shredding into bite-size pieces.

Melt the butter in a small sauté pan over medium heat. Add the shallot and cook for 3 minutes until softened. Add the shiitakes and sauté for 2 to 3 minutes until soft. Season with salt and pepper to taste.

Scatter one half of the mozzarella over 1 tortilla. Top with the chicken, the mushroom mixture, sesame seeds, and the remaining cheese. Cover with the second tortilla and press down lightly.

Heat a pan or griddle over medium heat, and cook the quesadilla for 2 to 3 minutes on each side until it lightly browns and the cheese melts. Remove it from the pan and cut into wedges. Garnish with the scallion slices.

Grilled Chicken with Roasted Red Peppers and Spinach

This peppery grilled chicken marries well with the roasted red peppers. Try to take the time to roast your own peppers—the flavor is worth the extra effort! However, if you just don't have the time, go ahead and substitute good-quality roasted red peppers from a jar.

2	fresh (8- to 10-inch) flour tortillas
1	tablespoon olive oil
1/2	(4-ounce) chicken breast, boneless and skinless
1	tablespoon freshly ground black pepper
3	ounces Monterey Jack cheese, shredded
1/2	cup chopped roasted red peppers
1/3	cup chopped, blanched spinach
2	tablespoons chopped scallions
1/2	cup Avocado Salsa for garnish (page 149)

Preheat your grill.

Brush the oil on both sides of the chicken breast, and coat with the ground pepper, patting lightly to ensure that the pepper sticks to the chicken. Grill over a medium fire for 3 to 4 minutes per side until no longer pink inside. Set aside to cool slightly before shredding into bite-size pieces.

Scatter one half of the Monterey Jack over 1 tortilla. Spread the shredded chicken evenly over the tortilla, followed by the red peppers, spinach, scallions, and the remaining cheese. Cover with the second tortilla and press down lightly.

Heat a pan or griddle over medium heat, and cook the quesadilla for 2 to 3 minutes on each side until it lightly browns and the cheese melts. Remove it from the pan and cut into wedges. Garnish with the Avocado Salsa.

Grilled Chicken with Toasted Pecans and Goat Cheese

Make sure you use a high-quality natural goat cheese for this recipe. Combined with the toasted pecans, this is a particularly delicious—and simple—quesadilla.

2	fresh (8- to 10-inch) flour tortillas
1/4	cup chopped toasted pecans
1	teaspoon olive oil
1	(6- to 8-ounce) chicken breast, boneless and skinless Salt and freshly ground black pepper
3	ounces high-quality soft, natural goat cheese
1/2	teaspoon kosher or sea salt

Reserve one third of the pecans for garnish.

Preheat your grill. Brush oil on both sides of the chicken breast, season lightly with salt and pepper, and grill over a medium fire for 3 to 4 minutes per side until done. Set aside to cool slightly before shredding into bite-size pieces.

Crumble the goat cheese over 1 tortilla. Scatter the chicken over the cheese, followed by the pecans. Sprinkle the kosher salt over all. Cover with the second tortilla and press down lightly.

Heat a pan or griddle over medium heat, and cook the quesadilla for 2 to 3 minutes on each side until it lightly browns and the cheese melts. Remove it from the pan and cut into wedges. Garnish with the remaining pecans.

Grilled Chicken and Monterey Jack

A classic quesadilla!

2   fresh (8- to 10-inch) flour tortillas
2   tablespoons olive oil
1 ' tablespoon fresh lime juice
1/2 teaspoon high quality chile powder, such as ancho or pasilla chile
1   tablespoon kosher or sea salt
1/2 teaspoon freshly ground black pepper
1   (6- to 8-ounce) chicken breast, boneless and skinless
4   ounces Monterey Jack cheese, shredded
1/4 cup chopped chives
1   tablespoon minced fresh cilantro
    Salt and freshly ground black pepper
2   tablespoons sour cream for garnish
2   tablespoons Guacamole for garnish (page 150)

Combine the olive oil, lime juice, chile powder, 1 tablespoon salt, and 1/2 teaspoon pepper. Marinate the chicken in this mixture for 1 hour in the refrigerator. Preheat your grill.

Grill the chicken over a medium fire for 3 to 4 minutes per side until done. Set aside to cool slightly before shredding into bite-size pieces.

In a medium-size bowl combine the chicken with the Monterey Jack, chives, and cilantro. Season to taste with salt and freshly ground pepper. Spread the mixture evenly over 1 tortilla. Cover with the second tortilla and press down lightly.

Heat a pan or griddle over medium heat, and cook the quesadilla for 2 to 3 minutes on each side until it lightly browns and the cheese melts. Remove it from the pan and cut into wedges. Garnish with the sour cream and Guacamole.

Grilled Chicken
with Vidalia Onion,
Black Olives, and Pesto

The olives and pesto give this quesadilla a rich, full flavor. If you cannot get Vidalia onions, substitute the sweetest variety available.

2   fresh (10-inch) flour tortillas
4   tablespoons olive oil
1   clove garlic, minced
1   teaspoon freshly ground black pepper
1/2   teaspoon salt
1   (6- to 8-ounce) chicken breast, boneless and skinless
1/2   Vidalia onion, cut in 1/4-inch slices
1   tablespoon basil pesto
1/4   cup pitted and chopped black olives
3   ounces Monterey Jack cheese, shredded
1/4   cup Fresh Tomato Salsa for garnish (page 159)

Combine 3 tablespoons of the olive oil with the garlic, pepper, and salt. Marinate the chicken in this mixture for 30 to 60 minutes in the refrigerator. Coat the onion slices with the remaining 1 tablespoon of the olive oil. Preheat your grill.

Grill the chicken over a medium fire for 3 to 4 minutes per side until done. Set aside to cool slightly before shredding into bite-size pieces.

While the chicken is grilling, grill the onion slices until nicely tender and caramelized. Remove from heat.

Spread the pesto evenly over 1 tortilla. Top with the chicken, onions, olives, and Monterey Jack. Cover with the second tortilla and press down lightly.

Heat a pan or griddle over medium heat, and cook the quesadilla for 2 to 3 minutes on each side until it lightly browns and the cheese melts. Remove it from the pan and cut into wedges. Garnish with the Fresh Tomato Salsa.

Chicken, Pine Nuts, and Roasted Poblano

The slightly sweet flavor of pine nuts, combined with the smoky, mildly hot flavor of roasted poblanos and sautéed chicken makes for a delightfully modern twist on the traditional chicken quesadilla. Serve with guacamole or a black bean salsa.

2   fresh (10-inch) flour tortillas
1   (6- to-8 ounce) chicken breast, boneless and skinless
1/2   teaspoon chile powder (pasilla)
     Kosher or sea salt
     Freshly ground black pepper
1   teaspoon olive oil
1/2   cup finely chopped toasted pine nuts
1/2   cup shredded Monterey Jack cheese
1/4   cup shredded Danish fontina cheese
1/2   cup chopped roasted poblano chile (peeled and seeds and stems removed)
1/8   teaspoon hot pepper flakes (optional)
1/4   cup minced fresh cilantro

Preheat oven to 350 degrees F.

Sprinkle the chicken breasts on both sides with the pasilla (or another high-quality chile powder), salt and pepper to taste, and pat with your hands.

Heat the olive oil in a skillet over medium-high heat. Sauté the chicken for about 5 minutes per side until golden. Set aside to cool slightly before shredding into bite-size pieces.

In a medium-size bowl combine the chicken, pine nuts, Monterey Jack, fontina, poblano chile, hot pepper flakes, and cilantro. Spread the mixture evenly over one half of each tortilla, fold tortillas in half, and press down lightly.

Set the half-moon quesadillas on a baking sheet and bake until the tortillas start to brown. Remove from the oven and cut into wedges.

Smoked Duck, Shiitake Mushrooms, and Herbed Goat Cheese

When we are the lucky recipients of our friend's home-smoked duck, we find this quesadilla to be a great way to enjoy it. Of course, if you don't have a friend who smokes duck for you, you can buy duck from your butcher and smoke it yourself, or simply roast the duck and use it in this recipe anyway.

2   fresh (8- to 10-inch) flour tortillas
1   tablespoon unsalted butter
1/2 cup sliced fresh shiitake mushrooms
1   shallot, finely minced
3   ounces fresh herbed goat cheese, crumbled
1   smoked duck breast, boneless and skinless, sliced thinly
     and cut into small pieces
2   ounces mozzarella cheese, shredded
2   tablespoons minced fresh cilantro
     Salt and freshly ground black pepper
1/2 cup Avocado Salsa (page 149)

Melt the butter in a medium sauté pan over medium-high heat. Sauté the mushrooms and shallots until tender, about 5 minutes. Remove from heat and set aside.

Spread the goat cheese over 1 tortilla. Evenly scatter the duck and one half of the mozzarella over the goat cheese. Cover with the mushroom mixture and the remaining mozzarella. Sprinkle with the cilantro, reserving some for garnish.

Season with salt and pepper to taste. Cover with the second tortilla and press down lightly.

Heat a pan or griddle over medium heat, and cook the quesadilla for 2 to 3 minutes on each side until it lightly browns and the cheese melts. Remove it from the pan and cut into wedges. Garnish with the remaining cilantro. Serve with the Avocado Salsa on the side.

Turkey with Roasted Poblano and Sautéed Walnuts

This is a great recipe for that leftover Thanksgiving turkey or roasted chicken. If you are feeling a little fancier, try grilled chicken or roasted duck with the poblano and walnuts. No matter which poultry, this is a great flavor combination.

2	fresh (8- to 10-inch) flour tortillas
1	teaspoon olive oil
$1/4$	cup finely chopped walnuts
$1/2$	teaspoon fresh thyme or $1/4$ teaspoon dried
$1/8$	teaspoon red chile powder, such as ancho or pasilla
4	to 6 ounces dark and light cooked turkey, cut into small pieces
3	ounces Monterey Jack cheese, shredded
1	poblano chile, roasted, seeds and stem removed, and finely chopped
1	tablespoon minced fresh cilantro
	Salt and freshly ground black pepper
1	sprig fresh cilantro for garnish

Heat the olive oil in a sauté pan over medium-high heat. Add the walnuts, thyme, and chile powder and stir for about 2 minutes until the walnuts are lightly browned. Remove from heat and reserve 1 tablespoon for garnish.

In a medium-size bowl, combine the walnuts, turkey, Monterey Jack, poblano chile, and cilantro. Scatter the mixture evenly over 1 tortilla. Sprinkle lightly with the salt and pepper. Cover with the second tortilla and press down lightly.

Heat a pan or griddle over medium heat, and cook the quesadilla for 2 to 3 minutes on each side until it lightly browns and the cheese melts. Remove it from the pan and cut into wedges. Garnish with the reserved walnuts and the sprig of cilantro.

Pork Tenderloin Satay with Grilled Eggplant and Scallions

This recipe gives an Indonesian slant on the quesadilla. Satays are small pieces of poultry, meat, or seafood marinated in a spicy, sweet marinade then grilled. Here the chicken satay is paired with the mellow, smoky flavor of grilled eggplant.

2   fresh (8- to 10-inch) flour tortillas

Indonesian Satay Marinade
1/2   cup peanut oil
1/2   cup minced fresh cilantro
2   tablespoons tamari
1   tablespoon hoisin sauce
1   tablespoon molasses
1   tablespoon Indonesian chile paste
1   tablespoon grated fresh ginger
1   clove garlic, minced

1   (4-ounce) pork tenderloin, sliced on the bias
      into 1/4 inch slices
1   small Italian eggplant, sliced lengthwise
      into 1/4 inch pieces
2   tablespoons olive oil
      Salt and freshly ground black pepper
3/4   cup shredded Monterey Jack cheese
3   tablespoons chopped scallions
1/2   cup chutney, such as Major Grey's, for garnish

Combine all the marinade ingredients in a glass bowl or clear seal-top plastic bag. Add the pork slices and marinate in the refrigerator overnight.

Heat your grill, and grill the pork over a medium fire for 2 minutes per side. Set aside to cool slightly before shredding into bite-size pieces.

Coat the sliced eggplant with olive oil and season with salt and pepper. Grill over a medium fire for 3 to 5 minutes until tender. Remove from grill and set aside.

Scatter one half of the Monterey Jack evenly over 1 tortilla, topped by the pork, eggplant, 2 tablespoons of the scallions, and the remainder of the cheese. Cover with the second tortilla and press down lightly.

Heat a pan or griddle over medium heat, and cook the quesadilla for 2 to 3 minutes on each side until it lightly browns and the cheese melts. Remove it from the pan and cut into wedges. Garnish with the chutney and the remaining 1 tablespoon scallions.

NOTE: You can find Indonesian chile paste at gourmet specialty stores.

Pork Tenderloin with Goat Cheese and Green Peppercorn Sauce

We got the idea for this quesadilla while dining at a French sidewalk café in Old Quebec City. We loved the way the flavors of the pork, the fresh goat cheese, and the sauce melted together with each bite. Only the tortillas were missing for a wonderfully French-influenced quesadilla!

2   fresh (8- to 10-inch) flour tortillas
1/2 teaspoon canola or sunflower oil
1   (6-ounce) pork tenderloin
1   shallot, finely minced
1/3 cup dry red wine
1/2 tablespoon balsamic vinegar
1/4 cup beef stock
1/4 cup heavy cream
1   teaspoon Worcestershire sauce
1   teaspoon green peppercorns in water, drained
     Kosher or sea salt and freshly ground black pepper
1   ounce mozzarella cheese, shredded
2   ounces fresh goat cheese, thinly sliced
1/4 cup minced fresh Italian parsley for garnish

Preheat the oven to 350 degrees F.

Heat the oil in an ovenproof sauté pan over medium-high heat. Pan-sear the pork tenderloin on all sides for 2 to 3 minutes until lightly browned. Place in hot oven for 7 to 9 minutes until firm and barely pink inside. Remove the tenderloin from the pan and set aside to cool. Maintain the oven temperature.

Add the shallot to the pan in which you cooked the tenderloin and sauté for 1 to 2 minutes over medium-high heat until tender. Add the wine and balsamic vinegar and reduce by half. Add the stock, cream, Worcestershire sauce, and the peppercorns. Reduce again until you have a thick, creamy sauce. Season with salt and pepper to taste, and set aside.

Slice the pork tenderloin on the bias into 1/4 inch slices. Add the meat's juices to the green peppercorn sauce.

Scatter the mozzarella cheese evenly over 1 tortilla. Cover with the second tortilla and press down lightly. Place on a baking sheet. Top the sandwiched tortillas with approximately 1/4 cup of the green peppercorn sauce. Scatter the pork tenderloin slices over the tortillas, and top each with a goat cheese slice. Drizzle a little more of the sauce over the open-faced quesadilla.

Bake for 2 minutes until the cheese begins to melt. Remove from the oven, cut into wedges, and sprinkle with the chopped parsley.

Virginia Ham, Shiitake Mushrooms, and Ricotta Cheese

This is a cross-cultural quesadilla whose subtle flavors seem to melt in your mouth! Make sure you get a good-quality baked Virginia ham, sliced very thin. Feel free to use a lowfat ricotta cheese.

2	fresh (8- to 10-inch) flour tortillas
6	to 8 ounces baked Virginia ham, sliced thinly and cut into $1/2$ inch pieces
2	tablespoons minced fresh cilantro
$1 1/2$	teaspoons Asian sesame oil
8	to 10 fresh shiitake mushrooms, coarsely chopped
$1/3$	cup ricotta cheese
$1/3$	cup shredded fontina cheese
	Salt and freshly ground black pepper

Dice 2 tablespoons of the ham and combine with 1 tablespoon of the cilantro and a few drops of sesame oil. Set aside for garnish.

Heat the remaining sesame oil in a small sauté pan over medium heat. Add the mushrooms and sauté for 3 to 5 minutes until brown and tender. Remove from heat.

In a medium-size bowl combine the mushrooms with the remaining ham, 1 tablespoon cilantro, ricotta, and fontina. Season with salt and pepper to taste.

Spread the mixture over 1 tortilla. Cover with the second tortilla and press down lightly.

Heat a pan or griddle over medium heat, and cook the quesadilla for 2 to 3 minutes on each side until it lightly browns and the cheese melts. Remove it from the pan and cut into wedges.

Garnish with the reserved ham-cilantro mixture.

Grilled Chicken with Kalamata Olives and Creamy Havarti

This quick quesadilla balances the sharp, tangy flavor of the kalamata olives with the mellow creaminess of Havarti cheese. This quesadilla works well using red chile tortillas.

2   fresh (10-inch) flour tortillas
1   (6- to 8-ounce) chicken breast, boneless and skinless
1   tablespoon olive oil
1   teaspoon freshly ground black pepper
1/2 teaspoon salt
3   to 4 ounces Havarti cheese, shredded
1/3 cup finely chopped, pitted kalamata olives
1   tablespoon minced yellow onion
1/2 cup Roasted Tomatillo Salsa for garnish (page 154)

Preheat your grill. Coat the chicken breast with the olive oil, pepper, and salt. Grill over a medium fire for 3 to 4 minutes per side until done. Set aside to cool slightly before shredding into bite-size pieces.

In a medium-size bowl combine the chicken, Havarti, olives, and onion. Scatter evenly over 1 tortilla. Cover with the second tortilla and press down lightly.

Heat a pan or griddle over medium heat, and cook the quesadilla for 2 to 3 minutes on each side until it lightly browns and the cheese melts. Remove it from the pan and cut into wedges. Garnish with the Roasted Tomatillo Salsa.

Ham and Red Dragon Cheese

Here's a new twist on the classic ham and cheese sandwich. Red Dragon is a Welsh semi-soft cheese made with whole grain mustard and ale. Try a maple-honey ham, or any other high-quality ham, sliced thin. If you can't find the Red Dragon cheese, try Cheddar and add some whole grain mustard.

2   fresh (8- to 10-inch) flour tortillas
4   to 6 ounces Red Dragon cheese, shredded
4   ounces maple-honey ham, sliced thin

Spread one half of the Red Dragon cheese over 1 tortilla. Cover with the ham, followed by the remaining cheese. Cover with the second tortilla and press down lightly.

Heat a pan or griddle over medium heat, and cook the quesadilla for 2 to 3 minutes on each side until it lightly browns and the cheese melts. Remove it from the pan and cut into wedges.

Chorizo with Black Beans and Fire-Roasted Corn

Chorizo is a spicy Mexican sausage made with pork, chile powders, garlic, cinnamon, clove, and other spices. If you can't find it, substitute andouille. The flavors of chorizo, corn, and black beans work well together in a traditional way.

4	fresh (6-inch) corn tortillas
4	ounces chorizo sausage
1	ear fresh sweet corn, husk on (³/4 cup kernels)
¹/2	cup cooked black beans (page 14)
2	tablespoons chopped fresh cilantro
4	ounces Monterey Jack cheese, shredded
1	teaspoon peanut oil
1	serrano chile, sliced, for garnish
	Roasted Corn and Tomato Salsa for garnish (page 153)

Preheat your grill.

Slice the chorizo into ¹/4-inch-thick half-rounds. Heat a large pan over medium-high heat, add the chorizo, and cook until browned, about 3 minutes. Remove from heat.

Place the corn directly on the grill over a medium fire. Roast for about 10 minutes, turning several times, until done. Remove from heat, remove the husk, and scrape the kernels off of the cob into a bowl.

Combine the chorizo, roasted corn, black beans, cilantro, and Monterey Jack in a mixing bowl. Scatter this mixture evenly over 2 of the tortillas. Cover with the remaining 2 tortillas and press down lightly.

Heat the oil in a pan or griddle over medium heat, and cook the quesadillas for 2 to 3 minutes on each side until they lightly brown and the cheese melts. Remove them from the pan and cut into wedges. Place a slice of serrano chile on each quesadilla wedge, and serve with the salsa.

Beef Tenderloin with Roasted Corn and Anaheim Chile

Here's a quesadilla that is Southwestern through and through, but a cut above your local Mexican eatery's fare.

2	fresh (8- to 10-inch) flour tortillas
1	teaspoon olive oil
1	(4-ounce) beef tenderloin fillet, finely diced
1	teaspoon commercial Southwest seasoning mix (or 1/4 teaspoon *each* chile powder, paprika, cayenne, and ground cumin)
1/4	cup fresh sweet corn kernels
2	tablespoons roasted, seeded, stemmed, and chopped Anaheim chile
1/4	teaspoon crushed red pepper flakes
1	clove roasted garlic, minced
3	ounces Monterey Jack cheese, shredded
1/4	cup Cilantro Crema (page 163)

Heat the olive oil in a heavy pan over high heat. Add the beef and Southwest seasoning mix and stir-fry for 2 minutes until lightly brown. Add the corn, Anaheim chile, red pepper flakes, and garlic, and continue stir-frying for another 2 to 3 minutes until done. Reserve 2 tablespoons of the beef mixture.

In a large bowl, combine the remaining meat mixture with the Monterey Jack. Spread evenly over 1 tortilla. Cover with the second tortilla and press down lightly.

Heat a pan or griddle over medium heat, and cook the quesadilla for 2 to 3 minutes on each side until it lightly browns and the cheese melts. Remove it from the pan and cut into wedges. Drizzle the Cilantro Crema over the quesadilla, and complete the garnish by mounding the reserved beef mixture in the center of the quesadilla.

Andouille Sausage with Roasted Poblano and Cilantro Crema

A Cajun-Southwestern quesadilla that gives you the spicy kick of the andouille sausage tempered by the cool flavors of cilantro and sour cream.

2   fresh (8- to 10-inch) flour tortillas
1   (4- to 5-ounce) fresh andouille sausage
1/4 medium sweet onion (Vidalia, Walla Walla, or Maui), thinly sliced
1 1/2 teaspoons olive oil
     Salt and freshly ground black pepper
1   poblano chile, roasted, seeds and stem removed, and chopped (or 2 tablespoons canned chopped green chiles)
3   to 4 ounces Monterey Jack cheese, shredded
1   tablespoon minced fresh cilantro
1/4 cup Cilantro Crema (page 163)
     Cilantro leaves for garnish

Preheat your grill.

Place the sausage in a saucepan and cover with water. Bring the water to a boil and then remove the sausage. Puncture it in several places. Grill over a medium-hot fire until browned on all sides and cooked throughout. Remove from heat and slice into 1/4-inch pieces.

While grilling the sausage, coat the onion slices with the oil; salt and pepper lightly, then grill the sliced onion until nicely soft and caramelized. Remove from heat, and keep fire going.

In a mixing bowl, combine the sausage, onion, poblano chile, Monterey Jack, and cilantro. Spread the mixture evenly over 1 tortilla. Cover with the second tortilla and press down lightly. Grill over a medium fire until it lightly browns and the cheese melts. Remove from heat, slice into wedges, and drizzle the Cilantro Crema over the quesadilla. Garnish with a few cilantro leaves.

6

Vegetable Quesadillas

These vegetable quesadillas make great summer side dishes for backyard grilling. They also easily stand alone as a light vegetarian meal.

If you're not accustomed to grilling vegetables, you may want to buy a specially designed grate for grilling vegetables and other small items. Widely available and inexpensive, it will open up a whole new realm of cooking for you. To prepare vegetables, simply cut them into the desired size, lightly brush with olive oil, season, and grill.

We use a number of pestos in our vegetable quesadillas because they nicely complement the vegetables. As with quesadillas, you can get pretty creative in designing pestos that go beyond the traditional basil–pine nut variety.

You will notice that we love to use Vidalia onions in our recipes. To our taste, there is simply nothing like the sweet, caramel flavor of a grilled springtime Vidalia from Georgia. If you cannot get hold of Vidalia onions, sweet Maui and Walla Walla onions are also great.

Barbecued Vidalia Onion, Roasted Red Peppers, and Hickory-Smoked Jarlsberg

The smoky, nutty flavor of this special Jarlsberg marries well with the grilled sweet onions and red peppers. This is a great early summer quesadilla. Keep your eyes open for the hickory-smoked Jarlsberg. If you cannot find it, try a smoked mozzarella or Gouda.

2	fresh (8- to 10-inch) flour tortillas
1	large Vidalia onion
2	tablespoons olive oil
	Salt and freshly ground black pepper
1/4	cup hickory-smoked barbecue sauce
1/2	red bell pepper, roasted, seeds and stem removed, and chopped
3	ounces hickory-smoked Jarlsberg cheese, shredded
1	ounce fontina cheese, shredded
1/2	cup Roasted Corn and Tomato Salsa for garnish (page 153)

Preheat your grill.

Cut the onion into 1/2-inch slices, taking care to keep the rings from separating. Brush with the olive oil, and season with salt and pepper to taste. Grill over a medium-hot fire for several minutes, turn over, and brush with half of the barbecue sauce. Continue grilling until the onion rings are nicely caramelized.

Coat the surface of each tortilla with 1 tablespoon of the barbecue sauce. Scatter the onion, bell pepper, Jarlsberg, and fontina over 1 tortilla. Cover with the second tortilla and press down lightly.

Heat a pan or griddle over medium heat, and cook the quesadilla for 2 to 3 minutes on each side until it lightly browns and the cheese melts. Remove it from the pan and cut into wedges. Serve with the salsa.

Grilled Zucchini with Vidalia Onion, Roasted Garlic, and Cheddar

Looking for something interesting to do with the summer's ubiquitous zucchini? Try this.

2	fresh (8- to 10-inch) flour tortillas
1	tablespoon olive oil
1/2	cup chopped Vidalia onion
1	clove roasted garlic, smashed
1	small zucchini, sliced thinly
1	serrano chile, seeds and stem removed, and minced
4	to 6 ounces Cheddar cheese, shredded
2	tablespoons minced fresh cilantro
	Salt and freshly ground black pepper
1/2	cup Roasted Tomatillo Salsa for garnish (page 154)
1/2	cup sour cream for garnish

Heat the olive oil in a small sauté pan over medium-high heat. Add the onion, garlic, and zucchini, and sauté for 2 to 3 minutes. Add the chile and continue to sauté for an additional minute. Remove from heat and mix with the Cheddar and cilantro. Season with salt and pepper to taste.

Scatter the zucchini mixture evenly over 1 tortilla. Cover with the second tortilla and press down lightly.

Heat a pan or griddle over medium heat, and cook the quesadilla for 2 to 3 minutes on each side until it lightly browns and the cheese melts. Remove it from the pan and cut into wedges. Serve with the salsa and sour cream.

Grilled Japanese Eggplant with Sun-Dried Tomato and Roasted Garlic Pesto

Japanese eggplants are smaller and have fewer seeds than the larger varieties. If you can't find Japanese eggplant, substitute a small Italian eggplant.

2   fresh (8- to 10-inch) flour tortillas
1   Japanese eggplant
1   tablespoon olive oil
    Salt and freshly ground black pepper
4   ounces white Cheddar cheese, shredded
3   tablespoons Sun-Dried Tomato and Roasted
    Garlic Pesto (page 160)

Preheat your grill.

Cut the eggplant lengthwise into 1/4-inch slices. Coat with the olive oil, then season with salt and pepper to taste. Grill over a medium-hot fire until nicely caramelized but not burned. Remove from heat.

Scatter half of the Cheddar over 1 tortilla. Lay the eggplant over the cheese, one end pointing toward the middle, like the spokes of a wheel. Cover with the remaining cheese. Spread 2 tablespoons of the pesto over the second tortilla. Place on top of the cheese, pesto-side down, and press down lightly.

Heat a pan or griddle over medium heat, and cook the quesadilla for 2 to 3 minutes on each side until it lightly browns and the cheese melts. Remove it from the pan and cut into wedges. Garnish at the center with the remaining tablespoon of the pesto, and serve.

Red Potatoes, Onion, and Roasted Corn with Fontina

Potato-onion quesadillas are a traditional Mexican specialty. This adaptation adds roasted corn and Danish fontina cheese for a great taste combination.

2	fresh (8- to 10-inch) flour tortillas
2	small red bliss potatoes (about 6 ounces)
1	cup sliced sweet onion (Vidalia, Walla Walla, or Maui)
1	clove garlic, roasted and minced
1/2	cup fresh sweet corn (about 1 ear)
2	tablespoons unsalted butter
2	ounces Danish fontina cheese, shredded
	Salt and freshly ground black pepper
1/4	cup sour cream for garnish

Cut the potatoes into small pieces, leaving the skins on. Cover with salted water and boil until cooked through, about 7 to 10 minutes. Remove from heat, drain, and set aside.

Sauté the onion, garlic, and corn in 1 tablespoon of the butter until the onions and corn are browned lightly. Remove from heat and combine in a medium-size bowl with the potatoes, fontina, and remaining 1 tablespoon butter. Season with salt and pepper to taste. Mash slightly.

Spread the mixture over half of each tortilla, folding the other half over to create a half-moon shape. Heat a pan or griddle over medium heat, and cook both quesadillas for 2 to 3 minutes on each side until they lightly brown and the cheese melts. Remove them from the pan and cut into wedges. Garnish with the sour cream.

Broccoli, Gorgonzola Cheese, and Sun-Dried Tomato and Roasted Garlic Pesto

Here's another way to use this fabulous pesto in a quesadilla. Once you've made a supply of the pesto, this is a quick-preparation meal you can make in minutes.

2   fresh (8- to 10-inch) flour tortillas
1   cup coarsely chopped broccoli florets
2   ounces mozzarella cheese, shredded
2   ounces Gorgonzola cheese, crumbled
2   tablespoons Sun-Dried Tomato and Roasted Garlic Pesto (page 160)

Preheat the oven to 350 degrees F.

Quickly blanche the broccoli florets in boiling salted water. Plunge into ice water, and then drain in a colander.

Scatter the mozzarella over 1 tortilla and cover with the second tortilla to form a sandwich. Distribute the broccoli, Gorgonzola, and pesto over the top of the tortillas to make an open-faced quesadilla. Place on a baking pan and bake for 5 for 7 minutes until the cheese melts. Remove from oven and cut into wedges.

Zucchini Pie #1

This recipe was inspired by an old Pillsbury Bake-Off winner that we used to make when we had a country house with a garden and lots of summer zucchini!

2   fresh (8- to 10-inch) flour tortillas
1   tablespoon unsalted butter
2   tablespoons finely chopped onion
1   small (4- to 6-ounce) zucchini, sliced thinly
2   tablespoons peeled, seeded, and chopped tomato
1/4   teaspoon salt
1/4   teaspoon freshly ground black pepper
1/2   tablespoon minced fresh basil
4   ounces mozzarella cheese, shredded
1   teaspoon Dijon mustard
1/2   cup Fresh Tomato Salsa for garnish (page 159)

Melt the butter in a sauté pan over medium heat and add the onion, zucchini, and tomato. Cook for several minutes until the zucchini is cooked and tender. Add salt, pepper, and basil, and remove from heat.

Combine the zucchini mixture with the mozzarella in a mixing bowl. Spread the mustard evenly over 1 tortilla. Spread the zucchini-cheese mixture over the second tortilla. Lay the first tortilla over the second, mustard-side down, and press down lightly.

Heat a pan or griddle over medium heat, and cook the quesadilla for 2 to 3 minutes on each side until it lightly browns and the cheese melts. Remove it from the pan and cut into wedges. Garnish with the salsa.

Zucchini Pie #2

This "pie" uses more tomato than the previous version, and takes on a smoky flavor from the smoked mozzarella. You now have a way to use up the summer's bountiful zucchini and tomatoes.

2   fresh (8- to 10-inch) flour tortillas
1   tablespoon unsalted butter
2   tablespoons minced onion
1   small (4- to 6-ounce) zucchini, sliced thinly
1   medium tomato, peeled, seeded, and chopped
1/4   teaspoon salt
1/8   teaspoon freshly ground black pepper
1/4   teaspoon dried basil
2   ounces smoked mozzarella, shredded
1   ounce Danish fontina, shredded

Melt the butter in a medium-hot pan. Add the onion and zucchini and sauté for 2 to 3 minutes. Add the tomato, salt, pepper, and basil, and continue to cook for another 2 to 3 minutes until the zucchini and onions are tender.

In a medium-size bowl, combine the zucchini mixture with the mozzarella and fontina. Scatter the mixture over 1 tortilla. Cover with the second tortilla and press down lightly.

Heat a pan or griddle over medium heat, and cook the quesadilla for 2 to 3 minutes on each side until it lightly browns and the cheese melts. Remove it from the pan and cut into wedges.

Wild Mushrooms and Red Pepper with Creamy Havarti

Wild mushrooms are widely available in grocery stores these days. Use any combination of mushrooms that you like—shiitake, oyster, cremini, etc. You can also mix in some white button mushrooms with one or more of the wild mushrooms.

2	fresh (8- to 10-inch) flour tortillas
1	tablespoon unsalted butter
2	tablespoons finely chopped onion
1	clove garlic, minced
1 1/2	teaspoons minced fresh thyme
1	teaspoon minced fresh basil
2	cups sliced assorted fresh wild mushrooms
1/4	cup thinly sliced red bell pepper
1/4	teaspoon salt
1/8	teaspoon freshly ground black pepper
3	ounces Havarti cheese, shredded
2	tablespoons sour cream for garnish

Heat the butter in a large pan over medium heat. Cook the onion and garlic until transparent. Add the thyme and basil and cook for another minute. Add the mushrooms, red pepper, salt, and pepper. Cook for 3 to 5 minutes until the mushrooms are tender.

Combine the mushroom mixture with the Havarti in a medium-size bowl. Spread the mixture over 1 tortilla. Cover with the second tortilla and press down lightly.

Heat a pan or griddle over medium heat, and cook the quesadilla for 2 to 3 minutes on each side until it lightly browns and the cheese melts. Remove it from the pan and cut into wedges. Garnish with the sour cream.

Grilled Portobello Mushroom with Hickory-Smoked Jarlsberg

The texture and flavor of a grilled portobello mushroom can almost fool you into thinking you're eating a slice of tender beef! The smoky-nutty flavor of the Jarlsberg complements the mushroom well. This quesadilla goes well with any of the roasted salsas (pages 152 and 154)

2	fresh (8- to 10-inch) flour tortillas
1	large (or 2 small) portobello mushroom cap
1/4	large sweet onion (Vidalia, Walla Walla, or Maui), cut into 1/4-inch slices
1	tablespoon olive oil
	Salt and freshly ground black pepper
1	serrano chile, seeds and stem removed, and minced
1	tablespoon minced fresh cilantro
3	ounces hickory-smoked Jarlsberg cheese, shredded
	Cilantro sprigs for garnish

Preheat your grill.

Brush the mushroom(s) and onions with olive oil, and lightly season with salt and pepper. Grill over a medium-hot fire, turning frequently, until tender. Remove from heat and cut the mushroom into 1/4-inch slices.

Scatter the mushroom slices evenly over 1 tortilla. Scatter the onion, serrano chile, cilantro, and Jarlsberg over the mushrooms. Cover with the second tortilla and press down lightly.

Heat a pan or griddle over medium heat, and cook the quesadilla for 2 to 3 minutes on each side until it lightly browns and the cheese melts. Remove it from the pan and cut into wedges. Garnish with a couple of cilantro sprigs.

Red Pepper–Almond Pesto and Smoked Mozzarella

This is a great, quick way to use that leftover pesto you made over the weekend!

2   fresh (8- to 10-inch) flour tortillas
3   to 4 ounces smoked mozzarella cheese, shredded
2   to 3 tablespoons Red Pepper–Almond Pesto (page 162)

In a medium-size bowl, combine the mozzarella and pesto. Spread the mixture over 1 flour tortilla. Cover with the second tortilla and press down lightly.

Heat a pan or griddle over medium heat, and cook the quesadilla for 2 to 3 minutes on each side until it lightly browns and the cheese melts. Remove it from the pan and cut into wedges.

Marinated Vidalia Onion and Three Cheeses

Marinating the sweet Vidalia onion gives it a mellow caramel flavor. A fruit-based salsa such as our Peach Salsa (page 157) complements this quesadilla beautifully.

2	fresh (8- to 10-inch) flour tortillas
1/2	cup extra virgin olive oil
3	tablespoons balsamic vinegar
2	teaspoons Italian seasoning mix
1/4	teaspoon salt
1/4	teaspoon freshly ground black pepper
1	Vidalia onion, thinly sliced
1/4	cup shredded Monterey Jack cheese
1/4	cup shredded Danish fontina cheese
1/4	cup shredded Jarlsberg cheese
1/2	cup fruit salsa for garnish

Mix the oil, vinegar, seasoning mix, salt, and pepper in a bowl. Add the onion and toss. Cover with plastic wrap and marinate at room temperature for 30 minutes.

Heat a large sauté pan over high heat. Drain the onions and quickly sauté them for 2 to 3 minutes. Remove from heat. In a medium-size bowl, combine the Monterey Jack, fontina, and Jarlsberg. Scatter half of the mixed cheeses over 1 tortilla. Evenly distribute the onion over the cheese, and top with the remaining cheese. Cover with the second tortilla and press down lightly.

Heat a pan or griddle over medium heat, and cook the quesadilla for 2 to 3 minutes on each side until it lightly browns and the cheese melts. Remove it from the pan and cut into wedges. Serve with fruit salsa of choice.

Shiitake Mushrooms, Scallions, and Sesame

This quesadilla blends Asian and Southwestern flavors for a truly unique quesadilla.

2   fresh (8- to 10-inch) flour tortillas
1   tablespoon Asian sesame oil
1   clove garlic, minced
2   cups sliced fresh shiitake mushrooms
1/2 cup thinly sliced scallions
3   ounces Monterey Jack cheese, shredded
1   serrano chile, seeds and stem removed, and minced
1   tablespoon sesame seeds, toasted
2   tablespoons minced fresh cilantro
1   tablespoon tahini
1/2 cup Avocado Salsa for garnish (page 149)

Heat sesame oil in sauté pan over low heat. Add garlic and cook gently for 1 minute. Add the mushroom and scallion slices and continue cooking over low heat until the mushrooms become tender, about 3 to 5 minutes. Remove from heat.

In a medium-size bowl combine the mushroom mixture with the Monterey Jack, serrano chile, sesame seeds, and cilantro. Scatter this mixture evenly over 1 tortilla. Spread the tahini over the second tortilla and place tahini-side down over the first tortilla. Press down lightly.

Heat a pan or griddle over medium heat, and cook the quesadilla for 2 to 3 minutes on each side until it lightly browns and the cheese melts. Remove it from the pan and cut into wedges. Garnish with the salsa.

Grilled Zucchini with Black Beans and Roasted Red Peppers in Red Chile Tortillas

Grilling lends a smoky, delicious taste to zucchini, which pairs well with the black beans and sweet, smoky peppers. The red chile tortillas add just a little bit of heat. If you do not want to make your own red chile tortillas, go ahead and use plain flour tortillas and add a few shakes of hot sauce, such as Tabasco, to the filling.

2	fresh (8- to 10-inch) red chile tortillas (page 22)
1	(4- to 6-ounce) zucchini
1	tablespoon olive oil
1/4	cup chopped roasted red peppers
1/3	cup cooked black beans (page 14)
3	ounces Monterey Jack cheese, shredded
1	tablespoon minced fresh cilantro
1	serrano chile, seeds and stem removed, and minced
1/2	cup Avocado Salsa for garnish (page 149)
1/2	cup sour cream for garnish

Preheat your grill.

Wash and cut the zucchini lengthwise into 1/4-inch slices. Brush the slices with the olive oil and let rest for 15 minutes to absorb the flavor. Grill over a medium-hot fire until lightly browned on each side. Remove from grill.

Combine the red peppers, beans, Monterey Jack, cilantro, and serrano chile in a mixing bowl. Spread the mixture over 1 tortilla, cover with the zucchini strips, and top with the second tortilla.

Heat a pan or griddle over medium heat, and cook the quesadilla for 2 to 3 minutes on each side until it lightly browns and the cheese melts. Remove it from the pan and cut into wedges. Serve with the salsa and sour cream.

Spinach, Roasted Red Pepper, and Hickory-Smoked Jarlsberg

The hickory-smoked Jarlsberg blends well with the smoky flavor of the roasted red pepper, and complements the grassiness of the spinach. Continue the theme by serving with a roasted tomato or roasted corn salsa.

2	fresh (8- to 10-inch) flour tortillas
2	cups fresh spinach, carefully washed and shredded
$1/2$	red bell pepper, roasted, peeled, seeds and stem removed, and chopped
$1/2$	cup shredded hickory-smoked Jarlsberg cheese
$1/4$	cup shredded mozzarella cheese
$1/3$	serrano chile, roasted, seeds and stem removed, and minced
1	tablespoon minced fresh cilantro
	Salt and freshly ground black pepper
	Salsa of choice for garnish
$1/2$	red bell pepper, roasted, seeds and stem removed, and julienned, for garnish

Lightly blanch the spinach, drain well, pat dry, and set aside to cool. Combine the chopped red pepper in a medium-size bowl with the Jarlsberg, mozzarella, serrano chile, and cilantro. Season with salt and pepper. Sprinkle half of the cheese mixture on 1 tortilla, top with the shredded spinach, cover with the remaining cheese mixture, and top with the second tortilla.

Heat a pan or griddle over medium heat, and cook the quesadilla for 2 to 3 minutes on each side until it lightly browns and the cheese melts. Remove it from the pan and cut into wedges. Garnish with the salsa and julienned red pepper. Serve additional salsa on the side.

Sun-Dried Tomatoes, Goat Cheese, and Roasted Garlic

Use the marinated-style sun-dried tomatoes for this recipe, and a creamy, fresh goat cheese.

2	fresh (8- to 10-inch) flour tortillas
5	ounces creamy goat cheese
5	large cloves roasted garlic, mashed
1/2	cup chopped sun-dried tomatoes, moist-style
1/2	teaspoon freshly ground black pepper

Mash and thoroughly blend together the goat cheese and garlic. Add the sun-dried tomatoes and black pepper to the mixture. Reserve 2 tablespoons of the goat cheese mixture and spread the remainder over 1 tortilla. Cover with the second tortilla and press down lightly.

Heat a pan or griddle over medium heat, and cook the quesadilla for 2 to 3 minutes on each side until it lightly browns and the cheese melts. Remove it from the pan and cut into wedges. Garnish with the reserved goat cheese mixture.

Kalamata Olives, Roasted Green Chile, Roasted Red Peppers, and Provolone

The strong, tangy flavor of dark kalamata olives from Greece stands up well to the chiles and red peppers. If you can't get kalamata olives, try French niçoise or Italian-style dark olives. Try roasting your own red peppers, but if not, buy a jar of high-quality roasted red bell peppers.

2	fresh (8- to 10-inch) flour tortillas
1/2	cup kalamata olives, halved and pitted
3	ounces provolone cheese, shredded
1/2	cup chopped roasted red peppers
1/4	cup canned chopped green chiles
1	tablespoon minced fresh basil
	Salt and freshly ground black pepper
2	tablespoons fresh basil chiffonade (thin strips) for garnish

In a medium-size bowl combine the olives, provolone, red peppers, green chiles, and basil. Scatter the mixture evenly over 1 tortilla. Season lightly with salt and pepper, cover with the second tortilla, and press down lightly. Garnish with the basil chiffonade.

7

Dessert
Quesadillas

People don't usually associate quesadillas with dessert, but in fact they can be a light and tasty way to follow up a meal—even a meal of other quesadillas!

The best way to make any type of dessert quesadilla is to use homemade tortillas. You can flavor them, sweeten them, and make them thinner and more delicate than those purchased in the grocery store. Although we prefer to use butter for richer taste and texture, shortening or a nut-flavored oil, such as hazelnut, can be substituted. We like sweetened tortillas for dessert, but this, too, is a matter of preference, and most recipes will work just as well with plain tortillas. To reduce fat and calories, use lowfat cheeses.

Tortillas can be fried in butter and sugar for extra crispiness, but we leave them plain for most purposes. Although quesadillas are traditionally grilled, many of the dessert cheeses work better at room temperature.

Recipes for folded quesadillas work just as well for flat or open-faced quesadillas, and vice versa.

There are many more flavorings for tortillas than we list in the tortilla section. Experiment with your favorites!

Chocolate-Raspberry Cream on Chocolate Tortillas

This is a rich dessert. We recommend it for very special occasions.

Makes 4 quesadillas

8	fresh (6-inch) chocolate tortillas (page 27), warmed
1/2	package raspberry gelatin powder
8	ounces cream cheese, at room temperature
1	cup fresh raspberries, or frozen raspberries, thawed and drained
1/2	cup miniature chocolate chips
1	cup Chambord Sauce for garnish, below

With a hand-held mixer, blend the gelatin powder into the cream cheese. Carefully cut in the raspberries and chocolate chips. Cover with plastic wrap and set aside.

Place 4 of the tortillas on dessert plates. Spread the raspberry mixture evenly onto each tortilla, leaving a 1-inch border. Cover each with the remaining tortillas. Cut into quarters.

Drizzle with the Chambord Sauce and serve.

Chambord Sauce

1	cup fresh raspberries
1/3	cup Chambord liqueur (a raspberry liqueur)

In a blender, mix together the raspberries and liqueur. Makes 1 cup.

Chocolate-Hazelnut Spread on Orange Tortillas

This quesadilla has a very special, delicate flavor. It works wonderfully as a light dessert.

Makes 4 quesadillas

8   fresh (6-inch) orange-flavored tortillas (page 29)
4   ounces mascarpone cheese
1/4 cup Nutella (chocolate hazelnut spread)
3   tablespoons chopped sugared hazelnuts (*bresilienne*)
    (page 134)
    Chocolate syrup

Blend together the mascarpone and Nutella.

Place 4 of the tortillas on dessert plates. Spread Nutella mixture evenly onto each tortilla, leaving a 1-inch border. Sprinkle lightly and evenly with *bresilienne*. Cover with the remaining tortillas and press lightly to make them stick. Decorate with lines of chocolate syrup, parallel or crisscrossed. Cut into wedges and serve.

Almond Mascarpone, Sugared Nut, and Dried Cherry Quesadilla

Another light dessert! Mascarpone is a soft Italian cream cheese available in delis and specialty stores. You can also substitute by adding 2 teaspoons of heavy cream to 6 ounces regular cream cheese.

Makes 4 half-moon quesadillas

4	fresh (6-inch) kirsch-flavored tortillas (page 29)
6	ounces mascarpone cheese
2	tablespoons granulated sugar
1/2	cup chopped sugared nuts (below)
1/2	teaspoon almond extract
1/2	cup dried cherries

In a medium-size bowl mix the mascarpone, sugar, nuts, almond extract, and dried cherries. Spread the mixture evenly over half of each tortilla. Fold in half to make 4 half-moon quesadillas.

Sugared Nuts

3	tablespoons unsalted butter
2	tablespoons granulated sugar
1	cup chopped nuts (macadamias, peanuts, walnuts, pecans, or hazelnuts)

In a small saucepan melt butter over low heat and stir in sugar until it melts. Add nuts and turn up to medium heat. Stir until browned, about 3 minutes. Place on waxed paper to cool. Use, or refrigerate in an airtight container for up to four months.

Cinnamon-Almond Open-Faced Quesadilla

Although there is no cheese in this quesadilla, it was too good to leave out. You can substitute the almond paste with 3/4 cup almond-sweetened mascarpone if you prefer.

Makes 4 open-faced quesadillas

4	fresh (6-inch) flour tortillas
1/2	cup almond paste
1/4	cup warm water
1/4	cup confectioners' sugar
	Ground cinnamon

Preheat the oven to 350 degrees F.

In a food processor fitted with the metal blade, gradually blend together the almond paste and water. Add sugar and blend again to achieve a smooth, spreadable paste.

Lay all 4 tortillas on a large baking sheet and spread the almond mixture on each, leaving a 1/4-inch border. Lightly sprinkle with cinnamon. Place into oven to warm, about 3 minutes, or longer if you want the quesadillas to be slightly crispy. Cut into quarters and serve.

Honey-Mango
Mascarpone Quesadilla

This is an exotic treat!

Makes 4 open-faced quesadillas

4   fresh (6-inch) shortbread tortillas (page 26)
4   ounces mascarpone cheese
$1/4$ cup honey
$1/2$ cup peeled, seeded, and diced fresh mango
$1/2$ cup Mango Coulis (below) for garnish

Blend together the mascarpone and honey. Carefully stir in th
mango pieces.
    Place each tortilla on a dessert plate. Spread each with
the mascarpone mixture. Cut each quesadilla into 4 wedges
and drizzle with a small amount of Mango Coulis.

Mango Coulis
$1/2$ cup peeled, seeded, and diced fresh mango
$1/2$ teaspoon fresh lime juice
$1/2$ teaspoon superfine sugar

Blend the ingredients in a food processor fitted with a metal
blade. Add additional lime juice or sugar to adjust flavor.

Apple and Brie
Quesadilla Pockets

This is wonderful harvest-time treat, or use as a light dessert.

Makes 4 half-moon quesadillas

4   fresh (6- to 8-inch) flour tortillas
1   large Granny Smith apple, peeled and finely chopped or
     sliced thin
2   tablespoons unsalted butter
1   tablespoon granulated sugar
1   teaspoon ground cinnamon
1/4 teaspoon fresh lemon juice
6   ounces Brie cheese at room temperature

Cook apples in butter in a medium pan until soft. Remove
from heat and add the sugar, cinnamon, and lemon juice. Stir
lightly, cover, and set aside.

Spread the Brie thinly on each of the tortillas. Spoon
apple mixture onto one half and fold over to form half-moon
quesadillas.

Heat a pan or griddle over medium heat, and cook the
quesadillas for 2 to 3 minutes on each side until they lightly
brown and the cheese melts. Remove them from the pan
and serve.

Pumpkin Pie
Quesadilla

This makes a nice substitute for a heavy pie on Turkey Day when your guests "can't eat one more bite."

Makes 2 large open-faced quesadillas

2	fresh (8- to 10-inch) flour tortillas
1	(16-ounce) can pumpkin purée
8	ounces Neufchâtel cheese at room temperature
3/4	cup granulated sugar
1	teaspoon ground cinnamon
1/2	teaspoon ground nutmeg
1/2	teaspoon ground ginger
	Whipped cream for garnish

Cream together the pumpkin and Neufchâtel, then stir in the sugar, cinnamon, nutmeg, and ginger.

Place each tortilla on a dessert plate. Spread each with pumpkin mixture, leaving a 1/2-inch border. Cut into wedges and garnish with fresh whipped cream.

NOTE: If you prefer to serve these quesadillas warmed, place them on a baking sheet in a 350 degrees F oven for 3 to 5 minutes.

Strawberry
Shortcake Quesadilla

A great summer favorite!

Makes 1 open-faced quesadilla

1	fresh (8- to 10-inch) shortbread tortilla (page 26)
$1/2$	cup heavy cream
2	tablespoons granulated sugar
4	ounces mascarpone cheese at room temperature
$1/2$	pint fresh strawberries, thinly sliced
2	tablespoons strawberry jam
	Additional whipped cream for garnish

With hand-held mixer, whip the heavy cream and sugar together until the cream peaks. Blend in the mascarpone. Carefully stir in the strawberry slices, being careful not to mash them.

Spread a thin layer of jam on the tortilla, then spread the strawberry-cheese mixture over it. Cut into wedges and garnish with the whipped cream.

Apricot, Orange, and Ricotta on Sugared Corn Tortillas

Although ricotta is not generally served as a dessert cheese, sweetening it makes it versatile, and its texture makes it quite suitable for this recipe.

Makes 4 quesadillas

8	fresh (6-inch) corn tortillas
1/4	cup honey
6	ounces ricotta cheese at room temperature
1/2	cup apricot jam
1/2	cup diced dried apricots
2	drops orange oil *or* 1/8 teaspoon orange extract
1/2	cup confectioners' sugar, sifted
3	tablespoons unsalted butter

With hand-held mixer, blend the honey into the ricotta cheese. Add the jam and stir until thoroughly blended. Stir in the apricots and orange oil. Set aside.

Dust a plate that is larger than the tortillas with the confectioners' sugar, and set near stove. Also set out a clean plate.

Melt the butter over medium heat in a large pan. Fry a tortilla on one side for 20 to 30 seconds to soften. Dip the buttered side of the tortilla in the confectioners' sugar, then set sugar-side up on the fresh plate. Repeat with all the remaining tortillas, stacking as you go.

Set four of the tortillas on separate plates, sugar side up. Spoon the apricot-cheese mixture onto the sugar side of 4 of the tortillas, leaving a 1-inch border. Cover with the remaining tortillas, sugar-side up, pressing slightly to make them stick. Cut into wedges and lightly dust with confectioners' sugar.

NOTE: The cheese mixture may be used at room temperature, or warmed for 15 seconds in the microwave before spooning onto the tortillas.

Fried Banana and Rum-Flavored Cheese on Macadamia Tortillas

You get a taste of the tropics with this recipe.

Makes 2 quesadillas

4   fresh (8-inch) macadamia tortillas (page 28)
2   medium bananas (or 1 large)
3   tablespoons unsalted butter
6   tablespoons brown sugar
6   ounces cream cheese at room temperature
1/4 cup rum
     Rum Sauce, below, for garnish

Cut the bananas in half lengthwise, then slice halves into 1/8-inch pieces. Melt the butter in a medium saucepan. Add 2 tablespoons of the brown sugar and stir until melted. Add the banana slices and cook until bananas are soft. Remove from heat.

In a medium-size bowl, use a hand-held mixer to mix the cream cheese, rum, and the remaining 4 tablespoons brown sugar. By hand, carefully stir in the banana mixture. Spread the mixture onto 2 of the tortillas and cover with the remaining tortillas. Cut the quesadillas into wedges and drizzle with Rum Sauce.

Rum Sauce

$1/2$ cup granulated sugar

2 tablespoons water

2 drops fresh lemon juice

$1/4$ cup dark rum

2 tablespoons unsalted butter

2 tablespoons heavy cream

Combine the sugar, water, and lemon juice in a heavy-bottomed pan and bring to a boil. Reduce heat and simmer until a medium-brown caramel forms (3 to 5 minutes). Remove from heat and blend in the rum, butter, and cream. Return to the heat and cook for a few minutes until the sauce is smooth.

Apples and French Gourmandise Walnut Cheese

This is a dessert variation of one of our appetizer quesadillas.
You must use freshly baked flour tortillas for this quesadilla.

Makes 4 half-moon quesadillas

4	fresh (8-inch) flour tortillas
1/2	tablespoon unsalted butter
2	tablespoons fresh lemon juice
2	tablespoons granulated sugar
1/8	teaspoon ground cinnamon
2	Granny Smith apples, thinly sliced
8	ounces French Gourmandise walnut cheese

Preheat the oven to 350 degrees F.

Melt the butter in a saucepan over medium-high heat.
Add the lemon juice, sugar, cinnamon, and apples. Cook until
the apple slices are tender and well coated with the sugar-
cinnamon glaze. Remove from heat.

Spread 2 ounces of Gourmandise cheese over each tortilla. Evenly distribute the apple mixture over one half of each
tortilla, fold in half, and press down lightly. Place the quesadillas on a baking sheet. Set in the preheated oven and heat
until the cheese melts, 3 to 5 minutes. Remove from oven, cut
each quesadilla into 3 wedges, and serve.

Peach-Almond Cheesecake Quesadilla

Adding a glaze to fresh tortillas makes them even more mouth-watering. Try this one when you are reaching for something extraordinary.

Makes 2 quesadillas

4	fresh (8-inch) flour tortillas
8	ounces cream cheese at room temperature
$1/4$	cup honey
2	tablespoons granulated sugar
$1/2$	teaspoon almond extract
1	cup peeled, seeded, and diced fresh peaches
	Peach Glaze, below, for garnish

In a medium-size bowl beat the cream cheese, honey, and sugar with a hand-held mixer until smooth. By hand, blend in the almond extract and carefully add the peaches. Spread the mixture evenly on 2 of the tortillas. Cover with the remaining tortillas. Serve at room temperature or refrigerate to slightly thicken the cheese.

To glaze the quesadillas, brush the Peach Glaze over them. Cut into wedges and serve.

Peach Glaze

3	tablespoons peach jam
$1/2$	teaspoon almond extract

Warm the jam over medium-hot heat until it liquefies. Remove from heat and stir in the almond extract.

8

Salsas, Sauces, and Pestos

Salsa is the Spanish word for sauce, and when most Americans think of salsa, they immediately conjure up an image of a fresh tomato salsa with a bit of a kick from chiles, onions, and garlic. In fact, varieties of tomato salsa—referred to as *salsa cruda, salsa fresca,* or *pico de gallo*—now outsell catsup as the condiment of choice for North Americans. But there are many more ways to make salsa than just with tomatoes, and we'll be providing you with a few of our favorites in this chapter.

When we refer to salsas, we generally refer to fresh, uncooked, somewhat chunky medleys of fruits, vegetables, herbs, and other ingredients. We use salsas as a garnish or side dish to pair with our quesadillas. Like our quesadillas, salsas combine a variety of flavors in creative ways that are sometimes hot, sometimes cool, sometimes sweet, sometimes sharp, and frequently a combination of the above. Salsas can be prepared quickly with a food processor, or they can be made carefully, so that each ingredient is diced into neatly proportionate pieces. When making salsas, feel free to experiment with the ingredients and the proportions—there are no hard-and-fast rules.

When we refer to sauces, we usually mean cooked, puréed blends of vegetables, herbs, butter, and cream. We generally use sauces in quesadillas that have a European influence, such as the Pork Tenderloin with Goat Cheese and Green Peppercorn Sauce.

Pestos can make a flavorful ingredient in quesadillas, or can be used as garnish in place of salsa. Like salsa, pestos are uncooked sauces that are easy and quick to prepare, and limited in variation only by the ingredients at hand. Although the classic Italian pesto is made with fresh basil, garlic, olive oil, pine nuts, and Parmesan cheese, we use pestos made with a variety of Southwestern ingredients such as cilantro, sun-dried tomatoes, and roasted garlic. As with salsas, feel free to improvise when making your pestos.

Each of our salsa recipes will make 1 to 2 cups. Pesto recipes yield about 3/4 cup. Most fresh salsas are best when consumed the day they are made. Fruit salsa should be eaten right away. Pestos can be refrigerated for up to four days.

Avocado Salsa

Makes 1–2 cups

No, Avocado Salsa is not the same thing as guacamole! Here we take care to dice rather than mash the avocado, and add unusual, non-guacamole ingredients such as rice vinegar and pumpkin seeds.

1	ripe Haas avocado, peeled, seeded, and diced
1/3	cup chopped fresh cilantro
1	serrano chile, roasted, seeds and stem removed, and minced
1	scallion, minced
1	tablespoon shelled pumpkin seeds
2	tablespoons extra virgin olive oil
1	tablespoon rice vinegar
	Salt and freshly ground black pepper

Gently mix the avocado, cilantro, serrano chile, scallion, and pumpkin seeds in a bowl. Whisk together the oil and vinegar in a measuring cup and pour over the avocado mixture. Briefly and gently mix, being careful not to mash the avocado. Season with salt and pepper to taste, and serve immediately.

Guacamole

Makes 1–2 cups

1   large ripe avocado, peeled, seeded, and cut into chunks
1/4   tomato, seeded and minced
1/4   cup seeded and minced red bell pepper
1/4   cup minced fresh cilantro
1   serrano chile, seeds and stem removed, and finely minced
1   tablespoon finely minced red onion
2   tablespoons fresh lime juice
       Salt and freshly ground black pepper

Combine the avocado chunks with the remaining ingredients in a bowl and mash together with the back of a fork.

Cilantro Pesto

Makes 3/4 cup

1 1/2 cups packed fresh cilantro
1/2 cup packed fresh Italian parsley
3 tablespoons pumpkin seeds or pistachios
3 tablespoons freshly grated Parmesan cheese
1 serrano chile, stem and seeds removed
1 clove garlic, smashed
1/4 teaspoon salt
2 tablespoons extra virgin olive oil
2 tablespoons fresh lime juice

In a food processor fitted with a metal blade, finely mince the cilantro, parsley, pumpkin seeds, Parmesan, serrano chile, garlic, and salt. Add the olive oil and lime juice, and process until blended to a paste.

Black Bean and Roasted Corn Salsa

Makes 2 cups

1	ear fresh sweet corn (about $^1/_2$ cup)
1	cup cooked black beans (page 14)
$^1/_2$	cup peeled, seeded, and chopped tomatoes
$^1/_4$	cup chopped fresh cilantro
1	scallion, sliced
1	serrano chile, seeds and stem removed, and minced
2	tablespoons fresh lime juice
1	tablespoon extra virgin olive oil
$^1/_2$	tablespoon balsamic vinegar
	Salt and freshly ground black pepper

Preheat the oven to 400 degrees F.

Husk the corn and cut off the kernels. Spread the kernels on a baking sheet and roast until they begin to brown, about 15 minutes. Set aside to cool.

Combine the roasted corn with the remaining ingredients in a medium-size bowl.

Roasted Corn
and Tomato Salsa

Makes 2 cups

3   ears fresh sweet corn
1   large tomato, seeded and chopped
1   roasted green chile (Anaheim or poblano), chopped
1   jalapeño chile, roasted, seeds and stem
    removed, and minced
1   clove garlic, roasted and minced
2   tablespoons minced onion
2   tablespoons minced fresh cilantro
1   tablespoon fresh lime juice
1   tablespoon extra virgin olive oil
1   teaspoon balsamic vinegar
    Salt and freshly ground black pepper

Preheat your grill.

Soak the corn, husks on, in cold water for 30 minutes. Grill over a medium-hot fire until lightly blackened, about 15 minutes. Fold back the husks and place the ears back on the grill, turning often, for 5 minutes. Remove from heat and allow to cool slightly.

Cut the kernels off of the ears of corn and place in a medium-size bowl. Mix in the remaining ingredients and adjust seasonings to taste.

Roasted Tomatillo Salsa

Makes about 1 cup

12	medium tomatillos
2	tablespoons finely diced red bell pepper
2	tablespoons finely diced sweet onion
1/4	cup chopped fresh cilantro
1	tablespoon fresh lime juice
1/2	teaspoon toasted ground cumin
1/2	serrano chile, seeds and stem removed, and finely minced
	Salt and freshly ground black pepper

Husk the tomatillos and rinse them under hot water. Place them on a grill over medium-hot coals until they are tender and begin to brown, or roast them in a 375 degree oven for 15 minutes. Transfer to a food processor and purée.

Combine the puréed tomatillos with the remaining ingredients in a bowl and blend thoroughly.

Mango Salsa

Makes about 1 cup

1   large fresh mango, peeled, seeded, and diced
1   jalapeño chile, roasted, peeled, seeds and stem removed, and minced
2   tablespoons fresh lime juice
1   tablespoon minced fresh cilantro
     Pinch *each* of sea salt, freshly ground black pepper, and crushed cardamom
1   tablespoon extra virgin olive oil (optional)

Gently mix all the ingredients in a bowl. Adjust seasonings to taste and serve.

Black Bean and Mango Salsa

Makes 2 cups

1	cup black beans, cooked and rinsed (page 14)
1	large fresh mango, peeled, seeded, and diced
1/2	red bell pepper, peeled, seeds and stem removed, and diced
1	serrano chile, seeds and stem removed, and minced
1	tablespoon minced red onion
2	tablespoons chopped fresh cilantro
2	tablespoons fresh lime juice
1	tablespoon unseasoned rice vinegar
	Salt and freshly ground black pepper

Combine all ingredients in a bowl. Adjust seasonings to taste and serve.

Peach Salsa

Makes about 2 cups

1 1/2 cups very ripe peeled, seeded, and diced peaches
2   serrano chiles, seeds and stem removed, and minced
1/2   red bell pepper, seeds and stem removed, and minced
1/2   cup chopped fresh cilantro
1   tablespoon fresh lime juice
1   teaspoon unseasoned rice vinegar
2   teaspoons honey

Mix all ingredients together in a bowl. Serve at room temperature.

Red Raspberry Salsa

Makes 2 cups

1   cup fresh red raspberries
1/2   cup seeded and diced fresh tomatoes
1   serrano chile, seeds and stem removed, and minced
2   tablespoons minced fresh cilantro
2   tablespoons raspberry vinegar
1   tablespoon fresh lime juice
1   tablespoon honey

Purée the raspberries in a food processor fitted with a metal blade or a blender and strain to remove the seeds. Combine the raspberry purée with the remaining ingredients in a bowl and mix until combined. Serve at room temperature.

Fresh Tomato Salsa

Makes 3 cups

2	tablespoons diced onion
2	cups seeded and diced tomatoes
1	large jalapeño, or 2 serrano chiles, seeds and stem removed, and finely minced
1/2	cup finely chopped fresh cilantro
1/4	cup unseasoned rice wine vinegar
1/4	cup beer or water
1	tablespoon fresh lime juice
1	teaspoon salt
1	teaspoon granulated sugar

Rinse the diced onion in a strainer under hot water; mix with the remaining ingredients in a bowl. Let sit for at least 30 minutes to allow the flavors to marry, and serve.

Sun-Dried Tomato and Roasted Garlic Pesto

Makes 1 cup

1   head roasted garlic
3/4   cup sun-dried tomatoes, moist-style
1/2   cup packed fresh cilantro
2   tablespoons pumpkin seeds or pistachios
1   serrano chile, seeds and stem removed, and finely chopped
1   tablespoon fresh lime juice
2   tablespoons extra virgin olive oil
2   tablespoons grated Parmesan cheese

Combine all ingredients but the oil and cheese in a food processor fitted with a metal blade. Process, adding the oil gradually until the mixture is smooth. Pulse in the Parmesan.

Olive Pesto

Makes 1 1/2 cups

1/2   cup pitted kalamata or niçoise olives
1/4   cup pitted California black olives
3/4   cup packed fresh Italian parsley
1   shallot, chopped
2   tablespoons toasted pine nuts
1   clove garlic, smashed
2   tablespoons extra virgin olive oil
1   tablespoon water
1/4   cup grated Asiago cheese

Place the olives, parsley, shallot, pine nuts, and garlic in a food processor fitted with a metal blade and process until finely minced. Add the oil, water, and cheese and process into a paste.

Red Pepper–Almond Pesto

Makes 3/4 cup

2   red bell peppers, seeds and stem removed, and chopped
1   shallot, chopped
1/2   cup toasted almonds
1   serrano chile, seeds and stem removed, and minced
1   clove garlic, roasted and smashed
1/4   cup extra virgin olive oil
2   tablespoons grated Parmesan cheese

Place the bell peppers, shallot, almonds, chile, and garlic in a
food processor fitted with a metal blade and blend until finely
minced. Add the oil and cheese, and process into a paste.

Cilantro Crema

Makes 1/4 cup

^{1}/4   cup sour cream
1   tablespoon chopped fresh cilantro
1^1/2 teaspoons water
^{1}/2   teaspoon fresh lime juice
      Salt and freshly ground black pepper

Combine all of the ingredients in a small bowl and mix.

Chipotle Crema

Makes 3/4 cup

$^1/_4$ cup chipotle chile purée (page 12)
1   teaspoon olive oil
$^1/_2$ cup sour cream
      Salt

Combine the chile purée and the olive oil. Add to the sour cream, 1 teaspoon at a time, until you achieve the flavor and color that you desire. Add a little salt to enhance flavor.

Roasted Garlic Crema

Makes 1/2 cup

4   cloves garlic, roasted
1/2   cup sour cream
5   dashes hot sauce, such as Tabasco
1   tablespoon water, white wine, or chicken stock
1/2   teaspoon fresh lime juice
1/2   teaspoon salt
1/4   teaspoon freshly ground black pepper

Combine all of the ingredients in a food processor fitted with a metal blade. Blend until the garlic cloves are thoroughly incorporated with the rest of the ingredients.

Index

Sesame-Ginger Shrimp with
  Spinach, 64
Sesame oil. *See* Oil, sesame
Sesame seeds, 80–81
  shiitake mushrooms, and
    scallions, 123
Shallots, 7–9
  in meat quesadilla, 78, 80–81,
    90–91
  in pesto, 161, 162
  sesame-ginger chicken with
    broccoli and, 78–79
Shiitake mushrooms
  with grilled sesame chicken,
    80–81
  scallions, sesame, and, 123
  smoked duck, herbed goat
    cheese, and, 90–91
  Virginia ham, ricotta cheese,
    and, 98–99
Shrimp
  grilled, sun-dried tomatoes, and
    ricotta, 66–67
  grilled, Vidalia onions, and
    Fontina, 60–61
  jerk with sun-dried tomatoes,
    Vidalia onion, and creamy
    Havarti, 59–60
  Sambuca, 58
  sesame-ginger with spinach, 64
  Smoked with Roasted Poblanos,
    Sun-Dried Tomatoes, and
    Goat Cheese, 62–63
  Vidalia onions, and Fontina,
    60–61
Smoked Duck, Shiitake Mush-
  rooms, and Herbed Goat
  Cheese, 90–91
Smoked Salmon with Herbed Goat
  Cheese and Capers, 42–43
Smoked Shrimp with Roasted
  Poblanos, Sun-Dried Toma-
  toes, and Goat Cheese,
  62–63
Sour cream, 34–35, 74, 85,
  106–107, 114, 124–125,
  163, 164, 165
Spicy Soft-Shell Crabs, Smoked
  Mozzarella, and Chipotle
  Crema, 68–69

Spinach
  grilled chicken with roasted
    peppers and, 82–83
  with sesame-ginger shrimp, 64
  in vegetable quesadilla, 126–127
Stilton, 3
  and sautéed walnuts, 46
  and roasted red peppers with
    grilled beef tenderloin, 76–77
Strawberry Shortcake
  Quesadilla, 139
Sugared corn tortillas, apricot,
  orange, and ricotta on, 140
Sun-dried tomatoes
  in appetizer, 34–35
  broccoli, Gorgonzola cheese,
    and roasted garlic pesto,
    and, 115
  cilantro, Havarti, and, with
    grilled swordfish, 50–51
  grilled Japanese eggplant with
    roasted garlic pesto and, 113
  grilled shrimp and Ricotta, 66–67
  jerk shrimp with Vidalia onion,
    creamy Havarti, and, 59
  pan-seared scallops with
    cilantro pesto and, 73
  and Roasted Garlic Pesto, 160
  in seafood quesadilla, 50–51,
    59, 62–63, 66–67, 73
  smoked shrimp with roasted
    poblanos, goat cheese, and,
    62–63
  in vegetable quesadillas, 116,
    117, 128
Swordfish
  grilled with roasted red peppers
    and cilantro pesto, 55–56
  grilled with sun-dried tomatoes,
    cilantro, and Havarti, 50–51
  grilled with sweet corn and
    tomato relish, 48–49

T

Tahini oil, 10
  in meat quesadilla, 78–79,
    80–81
  in vegetable quesadilla, 123
Techniques, 10
Tilapia, blackened with ginger,
  scallion, and red pepper
  sauce, 52–53

Vinegar
  apple cider, 10
  balsamic, 10
  marinade, 10
  rice, 10
Virginia Ham, Shiitake Mush-
    rooms, and Ricotta Cheese,
    98–99

W

Walla Walla onion, 7
  in meat quesadilla, 106–107
  in vegetable quesadilla,
    114, 120
Walnuts. *See also* Nuts
  French gourmandise, 32
  sautéed and roasted poblano
    with turkey, 92–93
  sautéed and Stilton, 46

Wild mushrooms, ginger, and
    fontina cheese·with grilled
    tuna, 54–55, 118
Wine, red, 96

Z

Zucchini, 8–9
  crab with grilled leek, roasted
    garlic crema, and, 71
  grilled with black beans and
    roasted red peppers in red
    chile tortillas, 124
  grilled with Vidalia onion,
    roasted garlic, and
    Cheddar, 112
  pie #1, 116
  pie #2, 117

International Conversion Chart

These are not exact equivalents: they've been slightly rounded to make measuring easier.

LIQUID MEASUREMENTS

American	Imperial	Metric	Australian
2 tablespoons (1 oz.)	1 fl. oz.	30 ml	1 tablespoon
1/4 cup (2 oz.)	2 fl. oz.	60 ml	2 tablespoons
1/3 cup (3 oz.)	3 fl. oz.	80 ml	1/4 cup
1/2 cup (4 oz.)	4 fl. oz.	125 ml	1/3 cup
2/3 cup (5 oz.)	5 fl. oz.	165 ml	1/2 cup
3/4 cup (6 oz.)	6 fl. oz.	185 ml	2/3 cup
1 cup (8 oz.)	8 fl. oz.	250 ml	3/4 cup

SPOON MEASUREMENTS

American	Metric
1/4 teaspoon	1 ml
1/2 teaspoon	2 ml
1 teaspoon	5 ml
1 tablespoon	15 ml

WEIGHTS

US/UK	Metric
1 oz.	30 grams (g)
2 oz.	60 g
4 oz. (1/4 lb)	125 g
5 oz. (1/3 lb)	155 g
6 oz.	185 g
7 oz.	220 g
8 oz. (1/2 lb)	250 g
10 oz.	315 g
12 oz. (3/4 lb)	375 g
14 oz.	440 g
16 oz. (1 lb)	500 g
2 lbs	1 kg

OVEN TEMPERATURES

Farenheit	Centigrade	Gas
250	120	1/2
300	150	2
325	160	3
350	180	4
375	190	5
400	200	6
450	230	8

ABOUT THE AUTHORS

STEVEN RAMSLAND is a healthcare executive and gourmet cook who has traveled extensively in the Southwest, California, and New Orleans, where he has sampled a wide variety of Southwestern cuisine. He has been experimenting with quesadilla recipes and serving them with great success at parties with friends for several years.

KATHERINE RAMSLAND is a professional writer. Among her ten books are *Prism of the Night: A Biography of Anne Rice*, *The Art of Learning*, and *The Vampire Companion*. She has also written numerous articles, and she reviews books for *The New York Times Book Review*.